FOLK CUSTOMS OF BRITAIN

FOLK CUSTOMS
OF BRITAIN

A GAZETTEER AND TRAVELLERS'
COMPANION

David MacFadyen
and Christina Hole

Illustrations by Val Biro

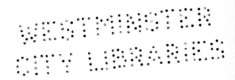

HUTCHINSON

London Melbourne Sydney Auckland Johannesburg

Hutchinson & Co. (Publishers) Ltd
An imprint of the Hutchinson Publishing Group
17–21 Conway Street, London W1P 6JD

Hutchinson Group (Australia) Pty Ltd
30–32 Cremorne Street, Richmond South, Victoria 3121
PO Box 151, Broadway, New South Wales 2007

Hutchinson Group (NZ) Ltd
32–34 View Road, PO Box 40–086, Glenfield, Auckland 10

Hutchinson Group (SA) Pty Ltd
PO Box 337, Bergvlei 2012, South Africa

First published in this edition 1983

Set in VIP Meridien by
D. P. Media Limited, Hitchin, Hertfordshire

Printed in Great Britain by The Anchor Press Ltd
and bound by Wm Brendon & Son Ltd,
both of Tiptree, Essex

British Library Cataloguing in Publication Data
MacFadyen, David
Folk customs of Britain
1. Great Britain – Social life and customs – 20th century
I. Title II. Hole, Christina
390'.0941   DA566.4
ISBN 0 09 151540 8

CONTENTS

St Margaret's Hope

Lerwick

Burghead

Stonehaven

Norham

Comrie

Alnwick

Whalton

Queensferry
Edinburgh
Lanark
Norha

Allendale
Durham
Irvine Biggar
Innerleithen

Workington
Warcop
Sedgefield
Whitby
Langholm
Jedburgh

Grasmere
Ambleside
West Witton
Scarborough

St John's
Ripon

Guiseley

Preston
Midgley
Barwick in Elmet
Dewsbury

Appleton
Liverpool Thorn
Castleton Haxey
Antrobus Buxton
Barlow
Anglesey
Blidworth
Youlgreave

Llangollen
Tissington Eyam
Ashbourne Wirksworth

Llanrhaedr-ym-Mochnant
Abbots Bromley
Bourne

Lichfield
Oakham
Little Walsingham

Atherstone
Aston on Clun
Meriden Hallaton Corby
Kidderminster
Knightlow Cross St Ives

Cardigan
Northampton Olney
Kings Caple
Cilgerran
Fenny Stratford
Great Dunmow
Colchester
Laugharne
Brockworth Yarnton
Tenby
St Briavels
Charlton-on-Otmoor
Oxford
Pencoed
Painswick East Hendred
Reading
River Thames
Southend-on-Sea
Hungerford
Bristol Aldermaston
Minehead
Great Wishford
Wotton
Biddenden
Guildford
Crawley
Hinton
Winchester Ebernoe
Shebbear Tatworth St George Tichborne Lewes
Marhamchurch Twyford

Padstow
Ottery St Mary
Kingsteignton Abbotsbury
Ideford
St Ives
St Columb Major
Helston

Jersey

St Bartholomew-the-Great, Smithfield
Law Courts, Strand, WC2
St Katherine Creechurch
St Clement Danes Church, Strand, WC2
Mansion House, EC4
Tower of London
Trafalgar Square, WC2
St James's Palace, SW1
Westminster Abbey
Houses of Parliament
Thames Embankment
Royal Hospital, Chelsea, SW3

INTRODUCTION

For some centuries now, diarists and commentators have been lamenting the decline of old magics and rituals in Britain, and prophesying that within a very few years, the customs that so delighted them and their forefathers would be gone forever. Perhaps this is more true of our own era than most; shifts in population have loosened old ties, mass entertainments have removed the necessity for people to make their own. Near-universal literacy has eroded folk memory and made it unnecessary that old rights should be remembered by a ritual. And young men returning from modern wars or from working in cities no longer feel the same enthusiasm for capering for the squire and his family on Christmas Eve as they did in the past.

Yet many ancient customs do linger on, sometimes adapted, yet in many ways unchanged, as tenacious as the yearly cycle of children's games. In the last few decades, some have been revived, often through the efforts of an energetic vicar and parish council. The Pancake Race at Olney, Buckinghamshire, is a good example of this. Almost forgotten, it received a new lease of life after the Second World War and now the race is run not only in Olney but on the other side of the Atlantic as well.

Even so, it is sometimes difficult to understand why contemporary men and women still feel the need to dress up in extraordinary clothes at set intervals and prance about the streets. The reasons are many, and run deep. To take part in such a ritual, or to ensure its continuance, fosters a sense of community, and newcomers to a village, perhaps former city dwellers, embrace its customs with just as much enthusiasm as the natives because that makes them feel that they, too, belong. Some customs also reinforce pride in a locality and help to recall a brave past or rights hard won. The annual forest walk at Great Wishford, for instance, reminds the world of the villagers' rights to gather wood, while the yearly rides in the Scottish Borders commemorate the days when every man and woman had to be prepared to fight for life and property against bands of marauding moss-troopers. Then, too, to be invited to take part in a ritual, particularly if it is a unique and famous one, such as the Obby Oss celebrations at Padstow, the Furry at Helston, or the doling out of Royal Maundy Money, is considered to be a great honour, and a mark of esteem in the community.

But the greatest attraction of all is tradition, the wish to ensure the perpetuity of things, and it is from precisely this desire that our most ancient customs spring. To our distant and pagan ancestors, such rites were a matter of life and death. Without them, how could they be sure that the sun would return in the spring to warm the seed in the ground and germinate new life? In the dark nights of winter, bonfires were lit on hilltops to remind the sun of its promise, and sacrifice was called for. Usually this was corn or a domestic animal burned, or returned to the earth that gave it birth, but occasionally, if times were desperate, a king or a champion might be called upon to die for his people, and his blood poured on the fields to make them productive again. Later, such extreme measures were replaced by ritualized dances or plays, but always the theme remained the same – death and rebirth, the triumph of spring over winter – and it remains still in many of our most cherished folk customs. Bonfires still blaze as the nights draw in, even if they supposedly celebrate Hallowe'en or the capture of Guy Fawkes, while at Antrobus and Marshfield and many other places in Britain, the old rituals are re-enacted in the form of mummers' plays. Though they vary in detail, the central plot is generally the same – a fight between two champions, one of whom is killed. A third performer then appears and resurrects the fallen hero – who in the play might be named Saint George or Lord Nelson. The name is unimportant; what matters is that life has defeated death and the cycle of the seasons will continue.

Of even greater antiquity than the mummers' plays may be the Abbots Bromley Horn Dance; figures very much like the horn-carrying dancers can be found in prehistoric cave art, and it is possible that the ceremony has its origins in a Stone Age hunting ritual. Other ancient ceremonies include the wild games of football that are played at various places at Shrovetide. Some scholars believe that these may have their origins in some form of sun-worship.

Some of our customs are of much more recent origin. These include the ceremonies stemming from charities that various kind souls instituted to supplement the income of the poor of their neighbourhoods. Often the donors insisted in their wills that the recipients perform some act – reciting the catechism, picking the money off their benefactor's tomb, or the like – to qualify for payment. Such charities occur in many parts of the country; the Knillian at St Ives and the Butterworth Dole in London are among the best known. In many cases, the purchasing power of the payment has so deteriorated that the ceremony is only maintained for the sake of tradition. Other customs too, such as the daily horn-blowing at Ripon, have long outlived their original purpose, but no one would dream of discarding them.

Other jealously guarded ceremonies are those that safeguard ancient rights, whether of parish, manor, town or trade guild. Beating the Bounds is a regular annual event in many places, and delightful quit-rent ceremonies, such as that of Knolly's Rose in London, are still enacted with great pomp and reverence each year up and down the country. Swan Upping on the Thames is a typical and picturesque affirmation of guilds' rights, while the town of Hungerford, in establishing its claims to free fishing in the Kennet River at its Hocktide Festival, reflects how such freedoms are cherished by many old British towns and villages.

Though it cannot be denied that a large number of our customs are lost now and forgotten, almost as many go blithely on – fairs and feasts, for example, whose original purpose is only vaguely remembered. Some of these cheerfully ignore the change that took place in the calendar in the eighteenth century and so, like Old Twelfth Night, are still celebrated eleven days out of step with the rest of the country.

There is still much for the folklorist, visitor or holidaymaker to enjoy in British tradition, and it is the purpose of this book to guide the reader to some of the festivals and ceremonies that can still be seen, and to tell the stories that lie behind them. At most of these events, visitors are welcome, but remember: the British take their fun seriously.

ENGLAND

ABBOTS BROMLEY, Staffordshire

The Horn Dancers

The Abbots Bromley Horn Dance is widely believed to be the most primitive dance in Europe. It is performed annually in this ancient village, which was once an important market town, on the Monday of the local Wakes Week – that is, the Monday after the first Sunday after 4 September. However, Robert Plot's *Natural History of Staffordshire*, published in 1686, says that the dance was performed 'within memory' at Christmas, New Year and Twelfth Day. This suggests that the dance was originally a Winter Solstice custom, but exactly when the celebration was shifted to its Wakes date is not known. Nor is it known precisely how old the dance is; both its age and origin are very uncertain.

One theory places its beginning in the twelfth century, during the reign of Henry I, after Abbots Bromley was granted some woodland rights in the Forest of Needwood. These rights are commonly believed to have concerned hunting, and the Horn Dance is said to have evolved as an expression of communal thanksgiving. There is, however, no evidence that any such hunting privileges were ever given to the people at that time.

The nature of the dance itself suggests a very much earlier origin, in pre-Christian times, in association with either hunting or fertility magic. The Horn Dance seems in any case to have been danced continually for many centuries in the area, with only occasional lapses, including one during the Civil War.

The horns used have their own mystery. They are undoubtedly reindeer horns mounted upon carved wooden deer heads, to which short poles are attached to make carrying easier. There are six pairs, of which three are painted white and the other three blue. The largest pair of horns has a span of 39 inches and weighs over 25 pounds. It is always carried by the leader of the dance. The others vary somewhat in weight and span, the smallest being 29 inches across and weighing 16½ pounds. The horns are kept in the Hurst Chapel in the parish church, and are collected from the vicar by the dancers on Wakes Monday morning.

No one knows where they come from, or when or who made them. Plot, in the seventeenth century, speaks of six 'Rain deer heads', which in his day were painted white and red, and had the arms of the three chief local families inscribed upon them. The carving of the wooden heads on which the horns are mounted seems to be sixteenth-century work, but nothing is known about the age of the horns themselves. Perhaps some ancient Norse settler in the district brought them as reminders of his country, though it is difficult to see why he should have burdened himself with anything so cumbersome. Or they may even be the horns of British reindeer, in which case they must date from before the twelfth century, when our native deer are believed to have become extinct.

The dancing team consists of twelve people. There are the six horn-bearers, the heart and core of the ancient ceremony, who carry their horns in such a way that they appear to be springing from their hearts. There is also a man dressed as a woman, supposed now to be Maid Marian, though the character may quite possibly be much older than that possible creation of romantic fiction. She wears a long dress reaching to the ground and a floating white veil, and carries an ancient wooden ladle in which collections are taken, which she beats with a short stick, equally old. Besides these, there is a Fool in conventional motley, a Hobby Horse, a Bowman, a boy with a triangle, and a musician who plays the accordion, as his predecessors played the fiddle and earlier still the pipe and tabor.

With the exception of the Man-woman and the Fool, the dancers wear a costume consisting of a flat cap, knee breeches and knitted green stockings, and a coloured sleeveless jerkin all in soft reds, greens, browns and gold. None of this is traditional. Formerly the performers wore their own clothes, decorated with ribbons and patches of coloured cloth; but in the second half of the nineteenth century, some local women designed a set of costumes faintly reminiscent of the clothes worn by the Morris dancers in the famous Betley window, and perhaps inspired by them. The new garments proved very popular, and since then they have

been remade and copied more than once. Although they are comparatively modern, they are very ornamental, fit in admirably with the spirit of the dance itself, and blend with the woods and green fields through which it passes.

On Wakes Monday, when the dancers have retrieved the horns from the church they set off on a 20-mile tour round the wide parish, which takes them nearly all day. On their way, they visit houses great and small, farmhouses and cottages, and dance outside them. It is said to be an omen of bad luck if they do not come.

With the horn-bearers leading, they silently enter the farmyard or the front garden and begin their ritual performance in a single-file circle. The leader breaks the ring by turning and passing between the second and third dancers, and the rest follow to form a loop. Then the six horn-bearers fall into two lines of three, dancing face to face. They raise their antlers and advance upon each other, as if to fight; they retire and advance again, seeming to lock horns; after repeating this movement once or twice, they cross over, passing left shoulder to left shoulder, then, turning, begin the whole sequence again from the opposite side. Meanwhile, the boy with the triangle beats time with his instrument, the Hobby Horse rhythmically snaps his movable jaws, and the musician plays the music of the dance on his accordion. The tunes he plays, like the clothes the dancers wear, are not old. One lovely old tune is known, but it is never played now. Two or three other customary melodies exist but are of no great age, and unfortunately there is a growing tendency to replace them with modern dance tunes.

When the set dance is over, the team

quietly follows its leader away to the next port of call. Eventually, the long round, with its luck-bringing visits, comes to an end and the dancers return to their home base, to dance again in the village street. At last, the horns are returned to the church's care until they are wanted again, and the rest of the evening is spent in well-earned revelry and feasting.

Abbots Bromley, a thriving market town in the fourteenth century, stands just south of Uttoxeter, 1 mile along the A518, then 5 miles down the B5013.

Nearest railway station: Uttoxeter.

ABBOTSBURY, Dorset

Garland Day

Old May Day, 13 May, is Garland Day at Abbotsbury, a long village behind Chesil Beach and about 12 miles south-east of Lyme Regis. For some days beforehand, the children of the village go round collecting flowers, which are then woven into garlands of traditional shape and mounted upon short poles. On Old May Day itself, the children carry the garlands about the village, stopping outside the houses to show them as luck-bringers to the house-holders, and receiving gifts of pennies or small silver coins in return. At the end of the day, the money is shared out and the garlands are laid round the war memorial as an offering to the memory of those whose names are inscribed upon it.

This is all that now remains of a cere-mony, undoubtedly of considerable age and said locally to run back for a thousand years, which was connected with the start of the fishing season. When Abbotsbury had its own little fishing fleet of a dozen boats or more,

each manned by a local crew and owned by local men, Garland Day marked the formal opening of the season. Every boat had a garland in its bow, made from flowers gathered by the seamen's children. At noon, all the gar-lands were carried to the parish church, where there was a service, and after-wards they were taken back to the boats. In the afternoon, the whole vil-lage made merry on the beach and played games and danced on the green below the castle. Then, towards evening, the boats put out to sea and when they were some way from land, the garlands were thrown overboard. As they floated away or sank, a song was sung or, according to some accounts, a prayer was said. All this was done to bring good luck to the fishing.

The ceremony was never omitted, and only after it had been performed by the crews of each of the boats was the new fishing season considered to have really started. Now, sadly, the fishing fleet has gone and the garlands are no longer carried out to sea.

Nearest railway station: Weymouth.

ALDERMASTON, Berkshire

Bidding by Candlelight

Candle auctions were well known and popular in the seventeenth and eigh-teenth centuries, and still take place in a few places today. In them, the lease of a piece of land, often belonging to the parish church or connected with some charity, is decided by the burning of a candle. At Aldermaston, in every third year, a meadow known as the Church Acre is auctioned in the parish hall at Easter. A pin is thrust into a tallow candle, about an inch below the flame, and bidding goes on until it falls out.

The last man to make his bid before this happens becomes the lessee of the land for the next three years. The rent tends to reflect current land rental values.

Though Aldermaston is chiefly associated nowadays with the nearby atomic research station, there are few signs of it in the delightful downland village. Aldermaston lies on the A340, 4 miles south of exit 12 of the M4.

Nearest railway stations: Reading, Newbury.

ALLENDALE, Northumberland

The Guisers

Burning the Old Year Out is an ancient practice in which communal bonfires are lit on New Year's Eve, or some other date near the Winter Solstice, in order to drive out old evils and bring fertility to crops and cattle in the coming year. It was once widespread and the tradition is still carried on in several towns and villages in Britain, including Allendale.

This Northumberland village boasts a particularly interesting New Year's Eve fire ceremony. Those taking part, known as the Guisers, go on their rounds of the village with blackened faces from about 8.30 p.m. onwards, while a band plays in the square near a central bonfire, as yet unlit. As midnight approaches, a procession is formed outside the Dale Hotel and the Guisers appear, carrying on their heads half-barrels filled with blazing tar and other combustible materials. They have to walk very quickly, for obvious reasons. When they reach the bonfire they circle it and each Guiser takes off his head gear and hurls it onto the bonfire, thus setting it alight. Immediately after midnight, they all set off first-footing all round the parish.

New Year's Eve is a great night for visiting and hospitality offered to friends and relatives by the people of Allendale.

Formerly, open house was kept for all and sundry, but so many strangers now come to see the fire ceremonies that such open-handedness is no longer possible.

Lonely Allendale is crossed by the B6295 and the B6303 that run north from Cowshill village on the A689; this links with the A690 from Durham.

Nearest railway station: Durham.

ALNWICK, Northumberland

Scoring the Hales

Shrove Tuesday football at Alnwick was formerly a street contest, like many other such games around the country. But for many years now, on the eve of Lent, it has been played in a field called the Pasture, between goals decorated with greenery and standing about a quarter of a mile apart. Rival teams of up to 150 men each are formed from the parishes of St Michael and St Paul. The ball is fetched from Alnwick Castle by a committee in charge of the proceedings, and is piped ceremonially to the field by the Duke of Northumberland's piper.

The game goes to the first team to score three goals, or 'hales', after which there is a wild scramble to get the ball off the pitch. Whoever manages to carry it off is allowed to keep it, but often has to swim the River Aln to do so.

Alnwick is just off the A1, about 20 miles to the north of Morpeth.

Nearest railway station: Alnwick.

AMBLESIDE, Cumbria

The Rush-bearers

In the Lake District village of Ambleside, on the Saturday nearest St Anne's Day (usually the last Saturday in July), a procession of adults and children goes through the town carrying garlands of flowers, as well as crosses, harps and other devices made of rushes. These include two great pillars of rush ten feet high or more. They go to the Church of St Mary the Virgin where a service is held, and afterwards the children are each given a piece of gingerbread. This ancient rush-bearing custom is a tradition handed down from the Middle Ages, when the stone or earthen floors of churches were strewn with rushes to allay the damp and cold. (For more information about the origins of this custom see *Grasmere*, page 32. In this village, only a few miles to the north of Ambleside, another rush-bearing procession is held.)

Nearest railway station: Windermere.

ANTROBUS, Cheshire

The Soul-cakers

On All Souls' Day, 2 November, or on its eve, small bands of children in some country districts of Cheshire and Shropshire still go souling, or soul-caking, from house to house, singing traditional songs and receiving gifts of money, sweets, fruit or cake. This practice is all that now remains of a once well-known custom in which, until at least as late as the 1860s, grown men and young lads, and poor people of all ages, used to take part.

Like the children of today, they made their rounds singing some version of the ancient souling song and hoping for the charity of their richer neighbours. Alms of any kind might be given to them, but one traditional gift was a specially made cake or loaf, usually called a soul cake but sometimes known by other names.

In Cheshire, the Soul-caking Play was enacted. This was a version of the Saint George play performed elsewhere at Christmas or at Easter, and the custom has been revived, after a long lapse, in the village of Antrobus. Included in the cast is a character unknown in other versions – the Wild Horse, or Dick, a man carrying a horse's head.

The origins of the Wild Horse lie in pre-Christian practices. In the Celtic calendar winter – the New Year – began on 1 November, at which time the spirits of the dead were believed to make a brief return to the world of the living, and offerings of food were left outside for them. Later, 1 November became All Saints' Day in the Christian calendar and the following day became All Souls' Day, when masses were said for souls in purgatory. The custom of leaving out food for the dead survived in the form of small spiced cakes – soul cakes – offered to children, although nowadays the offerings are more likely to be money.

The Wild Horse, possibly derived from the mount of the Norse god Odin, is among a cast which includes a character called the Letter-in, who starts the play by proclaiming; 'There is going to be a dreadful fight!' The Black Prince of Paradise, wearing a spiked helmet, is killed by King George, then resurrected by the Quack Doctor. Others in the cast include Old Mary, Little Dairy Doubt and Beelzebub, who uses a frying pan as a club.

Antrobus is in the rich Cheshire farming country that lies little more than 10 miles from the industrial centres of Widnes and Runcorn, linked by a fine new bridge across the Mersey. Leave the M6 at junction 20 and drive west on

B5356 to Stratton, then go south on the A559 for about 2 miles, where a side road on the left leads to Antrobus.

Nearest railway station: Warrington.

APPLETON THORN, Cheshire

Bawming the Thorn

This is a custom once regularly, but of recent years somewhat intermittently, observed at Appleton Thorn on or near 5 July (Old Midsummer Day). 'Bawming' is a dialect word meaning adorning or, according to some authorities, anointing; the thorn in this case is a living tree growing in the centre of the township, from which the village takes the second part of its name. Tradition says that the first thorn on this site was planted by Adam de Dutton in 1125, and that it was an offshoot of the Holy Thorn of Glastonbury. The present tree is very young: its immediate predecessor was blown down in 1965 and replaced by a thorn sapling planted on 25 October 1967.

The full ceremonies of Bawming Day include a procession through the village; the decoration of the tree's branches with flower garlands, red ribbons, posies and flags; and dancing round the thorn in a wide ring, together with the singing of 'The Bawming Song', a rather uninteresting ditty written in about 1870 by R. E. Egerton-Warburton of Arley, which may have replaced an older and more vigorous song. Afterwards there is a festival tea for the dancers; and the rest of the day is filled with sports, games and amusements of various kinds. In 1967 the new tree was too young to bear the weight of the garlands and flags, and so could not be bawmed properly, but this essential part of the old ceremony was preserved

by decorating the iron railings surrounding it.

Children are now the principal performers in this midsummer ritual, but formerly everyone in the village took part. William Beamont, a nineteenth-century local historian, has described how in his day and earlier, the thorn was honoured regularly every year, 'the neighbours paying respect by bawming and adorning it with flowers and ribbons, and holding a rural fete round it'. Many folk, said the same writer, came from elsewhere to see the garlanded tree and share in the merriment – too many, in fact, because the influx of crowds of strangers led to rowdiness and damage to property. For this reason and others, the custom was allowed to lapse. It was revived in a slightly altered form in about 1906 and again, after another lapse, in 1930. In spite of its intermittent performance in modern times, this is a most interesting ceremony, as it appears to be a relic of ancient tree-worship, and of the reverence once paid to the 'guardian trees' of early settlements.

The village of Appleton is barely 5 miles to the south-east of bustling Warrington, on the B5356 road – turn west at junction 20 on the M6 motorway. Nearest railway station: Warrington.

ASHBOURNE, Derbyshire

Up'ards and Down'ards

Shrovetide football, which may have pagan origins in the kicking about of the head of a sacrificed animal, is played on both Shrove Tuesday and Ash Wednesday at Ashbourne. The game begins at 2.00 p.m. on both days, and ends at 10.00 p.m. It used to continue until midnight, until in 1966 an amicable arrangement with the police reduced the 10 hours to 8.

The two goals are the mills at Clifton and Sturston, which are 3 miles apart, and separated by the quite sizeable Henmore brook, across or through which the players have to make their strenuous way. The ball is filled with cork and dust, so that it is heavy enough to discourage long kicks; the action is thus kept within a compact area. The teams, which like some country dances are for 'as many as will' are known as the Up'ards and Down'ards, according to whether the men who compose them come from north or south of the Henmore. Scores are rare!

Ashbourne, a most attractive market town, is on the fringe of the Peak District National Park, and is often called 'the gateway to the Peak'. Take the A52 north-west from Derby; Ashbourne is some 15 miles distant.

Nearest railway stations: Derby, Uttoxeter.

ASTON ON CLUN, Shropshire

Arbor Tree Day

An early summer custom which is clearly very much older than is locally supposed is the Arbor Tree ceremony at Aston on Clun. The Arbor Tree is a large black poplar standing by the roadside in the centre of the village. Once a year, on 29 May, it is dressed with flags suspended from long poles which are fixed to the main branches. These flags are left hanging during the year, and are renewed when Arbor Tree Day comes round once more.

It can hardly be doubted that this ceremony has its roots in the tree-worshipping cult of our Celtic ancestors, but local tradition explains it as a commemoration of the wedding of John Marston, then lord of the manor, to Mary Carter on 29 May 1786. The tree was dressed for the occasion, and it was said that the bride was so delighted by this pleasant sight that she gave a sum of money to enable the dressing to be repeated annually, on the same day, forever. No doubt the squire's marriage, which did in fact occur on that date, was celebrated in the village with rejoicing, but it is hardly likely that the Arbor Tree custom began as an eighteenth-century wedding compliment. What is more probable is that the bride's gift served to endow, and so preserve, a ceremony that was already firmly established at Aston on Clun when she first saw it. How long it had been observed there is uncertain; but it is perhaps significant that it was then, and is now, associated with Oak Apple Day, that anniversary of the Restoration of Charles II, who had hidden in an oak after the Battle of Worcester.

A few years ago, some newspapers reported that the twigs of the Arbor Tree were believed to have fertility powers and were much sought after by women desiring children. The twigs, they said, were asked for by, and sent to, brides in many parts of Britain and even farther afield though their effectiveness has not been ascertained. How this curious idea arose is not clear. It was certainly not supported by any old tradition that could be traced, and was probably one of those spurious pieces of so-called folklore which spring up from time to time. Nevertheless, it was the cause of a good deal of undesirable publicity which, in the short time that it lasted, even endangered the survival of the Arbor Tree ceremony itself. The latter was already threatened by proposals to remove the tree because, standing as it does at a cross-roads, it was thought to be an obstacle to traffic. Fortunately, however, no permanent harm was done; the Arbor Tree still stands and is ritually dressed with its flags as of old.

Aston on Clun, in the beautiful border lands between England and Wales, is a couple of miles along the B4360 road west of Craven Arms, which in turn stands on the A49 north of Ludlow.

Nearest railway station: Craven Arms.

ATHERSTONE, Warwickshire

Shrovetide Football

Every year on Shrove Tuesday, a free-for-all football game is played along Watling Street at the point where it forms the main street of Atherstone. The football used is decorated with red, white and blue ribbons and is filled with water to prevent it being kicked more than a few yards at a time. Promptly at 3.00 p.m. it is thrown from a window of the Three Tuns inn, and the game goes on until 5.00 p.m. However, at any time after 4.30 the ball may be deflated and hidden!

There are no goals and no recognized sides, although formerly two teams took part, one composed of Warwickshire men and the other of men from neighbouring Leicestershire. But during this century the inter-county aspect has been lost; now each man plays as an individual and does his energetic best to capture the ball for himself at the end of the game. If he succeeds in doing so, despite the determined efforts of all his fellow players, he not only wins the game but is allowed to keep the ball.

Atherstone is a couple of miles north-west of Nuneaton, on the great A5 trunk road, the Romans' Watling Street.

Nearest railway station: Atherstone.

BARLOW, Derbyshire

Well-dressing

At the village of Barlow, a water pump with a round stone basin is the scene of an annual well-dressing ceremony on the Wednesday after St Lawrence's Day – 10 August. During the ceremony large floral pictures are arranged in triptych form. The village claims the distinction of having kept up the custom without a break since the pump was installed in 1840, war years not excepted. (For more about the history of well-dressing in Derbyshire, see *Tissington*, page 82.)

Barlow is about 3 miles north-west of Chesterfield, on the B6051 road.

Nearest railway station: Chesterfield.

BARWICK-IN-ELMET, West Yorkshire

May Revels

The maypole is an ancient fertility emblem associated with the beginning of summer. It also represents a tree; at one time indeed it was a tree, brought in from the woods with ceremony on May Day and set up on the village green. In the darkness of the early morning, the young people went out and cut down a tall young tree, lopped off most of its branches, leaving only a few at the top, and brought the tree home to be adorned with flowers and garlands, and to serve as a central focus for their dances.

Philip Stubbes, a sixteenth-century writer who, like most Puritans, hated the maypole because he associated it with paganism and immorality, described the festivities as he saw them. In some parishes, twenty or forty yoke of oxen were used to drag in the tree, 'every ox having a sweet nosegay of flowers tied to the tip of his horns, and these oxen draw home this Maypole (this stinking idol, rather), which is covered all over with flowers and herbs'. He told how, when it was set in place and ready, the villagers began to 'leap and dance about it, as the heathen people did at the dedication of their idols, whereof this is the perfect pattern, or rather the thing itself'.

Sometimes the parish possessed a standing maypole, a permanent shaft which remained in position all through the year and was freshly painted and adorned when May Day came around. A few still stand – or rather their successors do – on the traditional site. The average age of a maypole is not much more than fifteen years, after which it begins to rot at the foot and has to be renewed. These 'permanent' poles are usually very tall; the shorter ones, around which children perform a plaited ribbon dance, do not belong to the English tradition – they are from southern Europe, and seem to have been introduced into this country by Ruskin in about 1888, as part of the somewhat poetic, if well-meaning, fantasy that luminaries of the Arts and Crafts movement had about the picturesque country idyll.

There is a permanent pole at Barwick in Elmet, near Leeds, which is 86 feet tall, and is taken down every three years, on Easter Monday, only to be set up again on Whit Tuesday. The arrangements are in the hands of three Pole Men, who are elected by others in the village. While the maypole is down it is repainted, or, if necessary, replaced, and its four garlands renewed.

It is one of a few that may have remained in position after an edict of 1644, which forbade maypoles throughout England and Wales. All but a few of the standing poles came down, though in some quiet places a few are believed to have been left defiantly in place, waiting for better times, though nobody dared to dance around them. Those times came with the restoration of Charles II, when most of the maypoles were re-erected to become the centre of festivities on May Day, or on that royal occasion, Oak Apple Day.

Barwick in Elmet is about 5 miles to the east of Leeds. Turn west off the A1 trunk road onto the A64, then south at Kiddal on a by-road which leads into the village.

Nearest railway station: Leeds.

BIDDENDEN, Kent

The Biddenden Dole

This is a charity of uncertain origin which is annually distributed in the village on Easter Monday. It is said to have been founded in the twelfth century by twin sisters named Eliza and Mary Chulkhurst who left 20 acres of land, still called the Bread and Cheese Lands, to provide an annual dole of bread, cheese, and beer at Easter for the poor of Biddenden parish. Tradition says they were born in 1100 and that they were joined together by ligaments at the shoulders and hips. When they were thirty-four years old, one died. The friends of the survivor besought her to save herself by having the ligaments cut, but she refused, saying that as they had come together, so they must go together. Six hours afterwards she too died.

How much truth is contained in this odd tale is very uncertain. The famous Biddenden cakes, which form part of the dole and which are baked from the pattern derived from old moulds, appear at first sight to support the story. Impressed upon them are the figures of two women standing so close together that they might well be united on one side, and having, apparently, only one arm apiece. The names of the Chulkhurst sisters are inscribed above their heads, and that of the village under their feet. On the apron, or skirt, of one is stamped '34', their age at death, and on that of the other, 'in 1100'. But this imprint, though it looks old, is not in fact old enough. Edward Hasted, the historian of Kent, said that no figures appeared on the cakes until about fifty years before he wrote in 1790, and that, when added, they were not intended to represent the donors but two poor widows who would be among those entitled to benefit by the charity. He dismissed the story of the joined twins as a tale without foundation, stating that the givers of the land were 'two maidens of the name of Preston'.

It is now fairly widely agreed that, whether the other details of the legend are true or not, the dates are wrong and that the charity was more probably founded in the sixteenth than in the twelfth century. Whatever the truth, the parish records show that the Biddenden Dole has been regularly distributed, at first on Easter Sunday and now on the following day, for more than 300 years. In 1646 and again in 1656, William Horner, the Puritan minister appointed in place of the sequestered Anglican rector, attempted to claim the Bread and Cheese Lands as part of the Glebe lands, but on both occasions his claim was defeated. Originally, the distribution was made inside the church, but in 1682 the Reverend Giles Hinton, then rector of the parish, complained to Archbishop Sancroft that the custom 'even to this time is with much disorder and indecency observed and needs a regulation by His Grace's Authority'. Thereafter it took place in the church porch, until the end of the nineteenth century. Then it was transferred to the Old Workhouse, built on the Bread and Cheese Lands in 1779 and now used as two cottages, which is still the site of the ceremony. A part of the Lands is now covered by a housing estate known as the Chulkhurst Estate.

One of the original gifts has disappeared from the dole. The distribution of beer is mentioned in records of the mid-seventeenth century, but after that no more is heard of it. The bread and cheese survive, however, and are still annually given to genuinely socially distressed claimants. Each person also receives a Biddenden cake in memory of the donors, and these cakes are also freely given to the many visitors who come to see the ceremony. They are really biscuits, and are decidedly more valuable as souvenirs than as food, since they are extremely hard, long-lasting, and practically uneatable.

Biddenden, a beautiful village containing old weavers' cottages and a medieval cloth hall, is on the A274, south of Maidstone.

Nearest railway station: Maidstone.

BLIDWORTH, Nottinghamshire

Cradle-rocking
On the Sunday nearest Candlemas Day, the ancient and lovely ceremony of

cradle-rocking is held in the parish church of Blidworth. An old wooden rocking cradle, decorated with flowers and greenery, is placed in the candlelit chancel, near the altar. The boy baby most recently baptized in the parish is presented by his parents to the vicar, who lays him in the cradle and, during the service that follows, blesses the child and gently rocks the cradle for a few moments. Then the baby is restored to his parents and the short rocking service ends with the singing of the *Nunc dimittis*.

This charming ceremony commemorates the Presentation of Our Lord in the Temple, which is remembered in the liturgy of the Church on Candlemas Day. This ceremony is believed to have been held in Blidworth as far back as the thirteenth century. It lapsed after the Reformation but was revived in 1923; since then it has taken place regularly every year. The village, said to be the birthplace of Robin Hood's Maid Marion and the burial place of Will Scarlet, is about 10 miles north of Nottingham, on a side road running west from the A614.

Nearest railway station: Mansfield.

BOURNE, Lincolnshire

The White Bread Runners
In 1770 Richard Clay of Bourne provided in his will for an annual gift of bread to the poor of Eastgate Ward, the cost of which was to be met by the rent of a certain piece of meadowland, now known as White Bread Meadow. This land has since been let every year at Easter by a form of auction in which bidding is only valid while two boys are running up and down a prescribed length of road.

How long they have to keep running depends upon the keenness of the competition and the number of offers. If a bid is made while they are on the move and is not capped by another before they return to their starting point, that bid stands; but if another is made while they are still running, they have to race off again. The auction ends only when no bid has been received during the double run to a fixed point and back again. The successful bidder then becomes lessee of White Bread Meadow for the following twelve months. The rental reflects the current rate for such acreage.

The boys are paid for their quite strenuous labours, and by custom all those concerned in the auction afterwards share in a supper of bread and cheese, spring onions and beer.

White Bread Meadow is just over a mile north of Bourne, where the Saxon hero Hereward the Wake was born in 1036. The town itself is on the A15, about 15 miles north of Peterborough.

Nearest railway station: Bourne.

BRISTOL, Avon

Whitsuntide Bouquets
When the Lord Mayor of Bristol comes in procession to St Mary Redcliff Church on Whit Sunday, and is received there with ceremony by the Bishop of Bristol, he enters – to a fanfare of trumpets – a church which is strewn with rushes and has a bouquet of flowers on every seat. This pleasant custom springs from the will of William Spenser, once Mayor of Bristol, who in 1493 left 'certain premises situate on the back of Bristol' to pay for a sermon (originally three, but now reduced to one) to be preached annually in that

church at Pentecost before the mayor and commonality of the town. Part of the money was allocated for rush-strewing and the ringing of bells, but the posies on the seats appear to be a later addition.

The thriving and ancient seafaring city of Bristol is easily approached, lying as it does at the intersection of the M4 and M5 motorways.

Nearest railway station:Bristol Temple Meads.

BROCKWORTH, Gloucestershire

Cheese-rolling

Cheese-rolling on Cooper's Hill, Brockworth, is an old Whit Monday custom which has now, like so many others, been transferred to the newly established English Spring Bank Holiday. In the evening of that day, the youth of the neighbourhood run races down the precipitous hillside for the prize of a cheese. An official, decked with coloured ribbons, hands a whole, circular cheese to the person who has been chosen to act as the Starter for that year, and slowly counts to four. At the word 'three' the Starter sends the cheese rolling and bouncing down the slope; at 'four' the competitors rush after it. Since the ground is rough and the gradient extremely steep, most of the runners measure their length more than once on the tussocky grass, and some roll a good part of the way, like their quarry, before the bottom of the hill is reached. The winner keeps the cheese, which is protected on its headlong flight by a strong wooden casing, and there are money prizes for the competitors who finish second and third. When the first race is over, other cheeses are released for further races, of

which there are sometimes as many as five or six, including one for girls.

It is said that cheese-rolling on this site dates from a very remote period, and that the villagers had to perform it to maintain their grazing rights on the common. Tradition says that the cheeses for these sports were formerly given by wealthier parishioners, and sometimes they still are; but nowadays a collection is usually made beforehand to pay for them and to provide money for other prizes and the general expenses of the festivity.

The course is run down that part of the very steep hill that is free from trees. At the head of it is a tall standing maypole which is decorated with flowers for the occasion. Before each race begins, the master of ceremonies, wearing a white coat and a top hat, makes an appropriate announcement. The annual ceremony has never been missed, even during the Second World War. When food rationing made the provision of several whole cheeses quite impossible, continuity was preserved by using a wooden dummy together with a very small piece of cheese.

Brockworth is only 2 or 3 miles east of Gloucester, just off the A417 near its junction with the A46 Cheltenham road.

Nearest railway station: Gloucester.

BUXTON, Derbyshire

Sacred Spring

Well-dressing takes place at Buxton on the Thursday nearest Midsummer Day. The custom is often said to have begun in 1840, but it is possible that during the Middle Ages, and perhaps even earlier, well rituals may have been performed by St Anne's Well, which was a healing spring in medieval times. It was Roman in origin and Roman relics have been found in or near it. No legend connecting it with Saint Anne herself is known, but at some time in the Middle Ages a statue was discovered in its depths, and was believed by the people of the time to represent Saint Anne. It may quite possibly have been a Roman statue, perhaps of a pagan water spirit, but it was piously enshrined in a chapel near the well and many miracles were ascribed to it. In 1538 the statue was swept away by Sir William Bassett, one of Thomas Cromwell's agents, together with all those 'crutches, shirts and shifts with wax offered', which had been left as offerings by grateful pilgrims. The chapel was forcibly closed and eventually destroyed, and although within the next forty years Buxton had become a noted spa, the cures achieved there were altogether medical, and had no religious significance. The modern well-celebration includes the blessing of two dressed wells and a festival for the whole town over which a Wells Festival Queen presides. (For more about the origins of well-dressing, see *Tissington*, page 82.)

Buxton is one of the highest towns in Britain, more than 1000 feet above sea level, but it is nevertheless sheltered behind still higher hills that surround it. It is little more than 20 miles to the southeast of the urban sprawl of Greater Manchester, along the A6 road.

Nearest railway station: Buxton.

which is obviously much older in origin than the event it commemorates and is probably a transferred May Day rite.

At about 6.00 p.m. a procession sets out to the music of a brass band and goes all round the village. It is led by the Garland King, a man riding a massive carthorse, and wearing over his head and shoulders a large wooden frame completely smothered in flowers and greenery. This is the Garland, which weighs over 60 pounds, and hides its wearer so effectively that only his legs are visible. On its top a separate crown of specially fine flowers is fixed, and is known as the Queen posy. Following the King in procession is another rider, who is called the Queen now, but seems originally to have been referred to simply as the Woman. Until 1956 'she' was always a man in female dress, veiled and riding side saddle, in the Man-woman tradition of many British folk rituals. In that year, however, the man who normally played the part withdrew, and the part was taken by a girl, as it has been ever since. Only time will show whether this break with long-established custom is permanent or whether on some future Garland King

CASTLETON, Derbyshire

Garland King Day

On Oak Apple Day, 29 May, the people of Castleton remember the Restoration of Charles II in 1660 in a ceremony

Day, the Man-woman will be seen once more in his/her old form.

At various points along the route, including the six inns of the village, the procession stops and the dancers perform. These are now schoolgirls dressed in white, but formerly it was the bell-ringers of the parish who danced, carrying oak sprays in their hands in honour of the king who hid in an oak tree. Before the present Garland Committee was formed at the turn of the century, the ringers not only provided the dancers but were also responsible for organizing and running the whole ceremony.

The procession ends at the church gates. The king rides into the churchyard, where the great Garland is lifted from his head and the crowning Queen-posy is detached from its place at the apex. Then the Garland is hauled by ropes to the top of the tower and fixed to one of the pinnacles. Once, it used to be left hanging for the rest of the year, or until it was destroyed by the wind and the rain, but nowadays it is taken down after a short time and stowed away until Garland King Day comes round. Finally the Queen-posy, which in the years before the First World War would have been offered to some admired local personage as a mark of honour, is deposited by the King at the foot of the village war memorial.

Castleton stands on the A625 road, about 7 miles east of Chapel-en-le-Frith.

Nearest railway station: Castleton.

CHARLTON-ON-OTMOOR, Oxfordshire

Dressing the Garland

In the parish church, a large wooden cross covered with clipped yew and box stands above the rood screen. It is known locally as the Garland, and twice in the year it is taken down, dressed with flowers and fresh leaves, and then replaced. The first of these renewals takes place on May Day, the second at the village feast on 19 September. On the May anniversary, little wooden flower-covered crosses are made by the children of the parish and taken by them to a service in the church and round about the village.

These customs have their roots in medieval times. Before the Reformation, two images, one of Our Lady and the other of Saint John, stood about the rood screen. On May Day, the former used to be carried in procession across the moor to the Benedictine priory at Studley. During the upheavals of the Reformation, the statues were destroyed, and the people of Charlton erected two green garlands in their place. An illustration in Dunkin's *History and Antiquities of Bullingdon and Ploughley* (1823) shows two hooped garlands, decked with evergreens and surmounted by a cross of slightly irregular shape, one larger than the other, and both curiously suggesting a roughly shaped human figure. By 1840, one of these had evidently disappeared, for in J. H. Parker's *Glossary of Architecture*, published in that year, a similar illustration shows only one. This remained in position until 1854, when the Reverend George Bliss, then rector of Charlton, had it taken away. That this was an unpopular move with his parishioners is proved by the fact that, as soon as he left the village, the garland, or another like it, was replaced.

Until the middle of the nineteenth century, both garlands while there were still two, and later the remaining one, used to be taken down for re-dressing on May Day and carried into the churchyard. From thence, preceded by morris dancers and a musician, they were taken into the open fields and about the village. The greater garland was carried, as the statue had been before it, across Otmoor to Studley Priory, by then a private house and now an hotel, while the smaller one was borne through the parish by women and girls. Dancing and singing made up the rest of the festival celebrations until 1857, when the processions and dances ceased, though the ceremonial garland-dressing still went on, as the dressing of the garland cross does today.

Charlton-on-Otmoor lies to the east of the A43, in what used to be a swamp, some 10 miles south of Bicester.

Nearest railway station: Oxford.

COLCHESTER, Essex

Oyster Feast
Colchester has owned the oyster fisheries in the River Colne since Richard I gave them to the town in 1186, and this is annually commemo-rated in the ceremonial opening of the season on 1 September, and in the splendid Oyster Feast in October, at which three or four hundred guests are usually present.

On the first day of the dredging season, the Mayor of Colchester in his robes of office, accompanied by mem-bers of the town council and, these days, of the Fishery Board, goes in a fishing boat from Brightlingsea into Pyefleet Creek. The Town Clerk reads aloud an ancient proclamation, dated 1256, which asserts that the fishery-rights in the river have belonged to Col-chester 'from the time beyond which memory runneth not to the contrary'. The company then toasts the Queen in gin and eats small pieces of gingerbread, after which the Mayor ceremonially opens the season by lowering the trawl and bringing up the first oysters.

The famous Oyster Feast is held in October in the Moot Hall. This is the last of the many civic feasts for which Col-chester was once renowned, all of which were held at the expense of the citizens of the town, and all of which were swept away by the ruthless broom of the Municipal Reform Act of 1835. The Oyster Feast perished with the rest, but after some four hundred years of continuous life it was too dear to the pride of the community to be allowed to vanish altogether. It was revived, and has since been held annually with much magnificence on or about 20 October. More than 12,000 oysters are said to be consumed by the guests on this great occasion of the town's year.

Colchester, which, in Roman times, was a capital city before London boast-ed a single house, is easily reached from Bury St Edmunds, Felixstowe or Cambridge.

Nearest railway station: Colchester.

CORBY, Northamptonshire

Pole Fair
The Pole Fair, or Charter Fair, at Corby takes place once in every twenty years, on Whit Monday. It was last held in 1982 and thus does not fall due again until 2002. The lively celebration, which has survived not only the natural changes of nearly four centuries but also the transformation of a village into a 'new town', albeit at the moment a depressed one, is called the Charter Fair

because it commemorates a charter granted to Corby by Elizabeth I in 1585, and confirmed by Charles II in 1682. By its provisions, exemptions from various toll payments, and from some jury and militia services, were conferred upon the people.

Local legends say that these privileges were given to Corby in gratitude for the prompt help once rendered to Elizabeth by certain villagers. During a visit to the nearby Kirby Hall as the guest of Sir Christopher Hatton, she went out riding. Her horse bolted with her and threw her into a bog, and from this awkward predicament she was rescued by some men working in the fields. What she did *not* bestow on the villagers, for this or any other service, was the right to hold a fair; but custom has added that name to the Whit Monday celebrations which, like many other country festivals, have long outlasted a number of true fairs in the neighbourhood.

The name Pole Fair has an even more interesting origin. It derives from a custom which clearly has nothing to do with any privileges granted by visiting royalty, and whose age and history are obscure. Before the festivities begin, the roads leading into the town are closed by strong barriers, and all travellers wishing to enter are required to pay a toll. If anyone refuses, he or she is carried off – astride a pole if a man, in a chair if a woman – to one of the town's three surviving stocks and made to sit in them until payment is forthcoming. The rate of payment is flexible and depends on what the 'victim' can afford, but from this cheerful custom there is no appeal. Corby people stand firm on their 'immemorial right' to act thus on fair day. Usually, it is true, recalcitrant captives are given a second chance to pay on arrival at the stocks, and before they are actually set in them, but that is the only concession allowed.

Nor is it only visitors from outside who are so treated. Anyone in the streets, male or female, old or young, is liable to be seized and similarly imprisoned unless due ransom is paid. Unwarned strangers may find it a little startling to be thus precipitated into the middle of a centuries-old frolic, but they can always escape a pole or chair ride by paying up promptly. Most people, whether visitors or townsfolk, enter freely into the spirit of the thing; it is by no means unknown for potential 'victims' to put themselves deliberately in the way of capture, for the thrill of sitting in the stocks, as their forefathers so often had to do for more serious reasons, and perhaps getting some friend to photograph them in that unusual position. Those who really object to such antics are well advised to keep away from Corby on the one day in twenty years when Corby remembers its ancient privileges.

The charter, with its list of benefits, is always read at the opening ceremony, to which the rector and town officials are carried solemnly and with dignity, in chairs. Corby is 5 miles or so north of Kettering, easily reached by way of the A43.

Nearest railway station: Corby.

CRAWLEY, West Sussex

Springtime Marbles

Marbles, like skipping, is one of the traditional springtime games associated with Good Friday. In Surrey and Sussex the anniversary was often called Marble Day because formerly it marked the end of the short marble season. This ran from Ash Wednesday to Good Friday, and ended on the stroke of noon on the latter day. Marbles was essentially a man's game, and was very seriously played by men and youths in numerous parishes all through Lent. It is still played on Good Friday at Tinsley Green near Crawley, where a championship match is held every year, outside the Greyhound pub. It is said to have been held there for the last 300 years.

Bustling Crawley is situated between the hush of St Leonard's Forest and the snarl of Gatwick Airport on the A23; Tinsley Green lies a little to the north.

Nearest railway station: Crawley.

DEWSBURY, West Yorkshire

Devil's Knell

The Devil's Knell, or the Old Lad's Passing Bell, is rung every year on Christmas Eve at the parish church of Dewsbury. The tenor bell is tolled once for every year that has passed since the first Christmas Day, one stroke thus being added every year. The solemn and lengthy ringing is timed to end exactly at midnight.

The Devil's Knell is said to be rung to proclaim Satan's defeat and death when Christ was born or, according to another version of the tradition, to protect Dewsbury people from the Devil in the coming twelve months. The precise age of the custom is uncertain, but it is known to have begun by the Middle Ages and the late thirteenth or early fourteenth century has been suggested as the most likely period. The custom is believed to have been instituted by Sir Thomas de Soothill, who gave the tenor bell to the church. Interestingly he is supposed to have done this, and to have required the bell to be tolled every Christmas Eve forever, in expiation for a murder which he had committed. Unfortunately little else seems to be known about him, except that he probably derived his name from Soothill, which is a small township within Dewsbury parish. Until very recently the tenor bell he gave to the church was known as Black Tom of Soothill.

Dewsbury is easily approached, being just off the M1 motorway between Huddersfield and Wakefield.

Nearest railway station: Dewsbury.

DURHAM, County Durham

Victory Remembered

On 29 May, the choristers of Durham Cathedral go to the top of the great central tower and there sing three anthems, facing towards the east, the north and the south – but not towards the west. No one knows why the western side is thus avoided, though there is a vaguely held tradition that once, long ago, someone (usually said to have been a chorister, but this too is unverified) fell from the west side and was killed.

Although the ceremony now takes place annually on Oak Apple Day, it has nothing to do with the Restoration of Charles II, nor was it always held on 29 May. It commemorates the battle of Neville's Cross, which was fought and won three centuries before Charles' reign. During the absence of Edward III in France, the Scots under David I invaded England and penetrated as far south as County Durham. On 17 October 1346 they were defeated by the English forces at a place on the Red Hills where, long before, a member of the great house of Neville had set up a fine stone cross. Much of the fiercest fighting raged around the cross, and from it the battle gained its name.

On the eve of the contest John Fosse, Prior of Durham, was commanded in a dream or vision to go on the next day to a hill near the cross, carrying with him as a banner one of the abbey's treasured relics, the cloth which Saint Cuthbert used to cover the chalice when he said Mass. In later years this became the battle standard of the Durham men, the famous Banner of Saint Cuthbert, which they carried to Flodden Field and during the Pilgrimage of Grace.

On that October day the Prior set it on the hill named in his vision. Then, with a small company of monks he waited on the high abbey tower, to see or hear whatever they could of the distant battle and to pray for the success of the English army. The monks also prayed for the safety of their prior. When victory was certain, they sang a joyous *Te Deum* and so made the good news known to the anxious townsfolk.

From then onwards, thanksgiving for that deliverance was offered annually in the same high place, first by the monks and later by the choristers of the cathedral who, with very few interruptions, have done so ever since. But in the seventeenth century this custom, like so many others, became absorbed in the spreading celebrations of Oak Apple Day, and now it is in May not in October that it is observed. Nevertheless in spite of the change of date, the original meaning of the ceremony has never been forgotten. It remains, as every Durham man knows, what it always was: the commemoration of a fourteenth-century victory, with only a coincidental connection with Restoration festivities.

The magnificent cathedral at Durham is centuries older than the commemoration ritual. Building was begun in 1093 and it contains the tombs of Saint Cuthbert and the Venerable Bede. With the imposing Durham Castle, built twenty years earlier, it lies now at the heart of a great university complex which encompasses most of the buildings in the old city centre. This beautiful and ancient county town lies directly off the A1(M) motorway, which runs past its eastern suburbs.

Nearest railway station: Durham.

EAST HENDRED, Berkshire

Shroving Song
Shroving, or Lent-crocking, at Shrovetide was a widespread children's custom until fairly recently, and in some parts of Great Britain it is not quite extinct. Like some other customs established at this time of year, it has added special names to the season, such as Lentsherd Night, Dappy-door Night, Lincrook Day, or Sharp Tuesday. On Shrove Tuesday, or on the day before, little bands of Shrovers visited various houses of the parish to ask for pancakes, eggs, cheese or anything else the householder could be induced to give them.

At East Hendred, a somewhat limited form of the old custom is kept up on Shrove Tuesday. The children no longer go round the parish, but punctually at noon they march up to Hendred House, the largest house in the village, singing a local variant of the traditional Berkshire Shroving song which ends with the lines

With the butcher up my back
A halfpenny's better than nothing!

On arrival at the house, each child is given a coin, and a bun, and then they all march away again, singing the same song, with its rather grudging suggestion of gratitude.

The charming Berkshire downland village of East Hendred lies just off the A417, about 4 miles east of Wantage.

Nearest railway station: Didcot.

EBERNOE, Sussex

Horn Fair Day

The Ebernoe Horn Fair takes place on 25 July, the Feast of Saint James the Great. It is locally said to have done so 'since time immemorial' and certainly, though its history and origin are both obscure, it does seem, allowing for occasional lapses, to be several centuries old.

Its distinctive features are the roasting of a horned sheep, and a cricket match. Every year, Ebernoe challenges some other village to a match; while this is being played, a horned sheep is roasted whole in a pit of embers on the edge of the common next to the cricket ground.

The head projects well over the end of the pit, so as to prevent damage to the horns. The roasting begins early in the morning on fair day, and while it con-

tinues visitors to the fair take it in turns to baste the meat, for this act is supposed to be lucky. When the sheep is cooked, it is decapitated. The rival teams enjoy mutton for their lunch, and at the end of the match, the head and horns are awarded as a trophy to the member of the winning team who has scored the most runs.

Ebernoe lies off the A283, about 4 miles north of the handsome seventeenth-century extravaganza of Petworth House, set in its perfect landscapes that Turner loved.

Nearest railway station: Pulborough.

EYAM, Derbyshire

Village of Heroes

In 1665 a box of infected cloth was sent from London, where the Great Plague was raging, to the village tailor at Eyam. It arrived in Wakes Week, at the end of August. Within a month, all in the tailor's house were dead of the plague except the trader himself, and the disease was spreading through the parish with appalling rapidity. The rector, William Mompesson, realized that little could be done for Eyam, but that the surrounding district could still be saved from disease if his parishioners would agree to abandon all ideas of flight and confine themselves voluntarily within their own boundaries for as long as the epidemic lasted.

Helped by his Nonconformist predecessor Thomas Stanley, who had been ejected from the living after the Restoration, he persuaded them all to consent to this truly heroic course, from which none deviated until the end came thirteen months later. No one was allowed to go more than half a mile outside the village, and no outsider was permitted to approach or enter it. The Earl of Derbyshire arranged to send food and other necessities, which were left on a stone far enough off to be safe for his messengers, and these were afterwards fetched by Eyam men still well enough to carry them. The church was closed but open-air services were held on Sundays in a hollow known as Cucklet Dell, where the rector preached to his stricken people from a rock.

The plague declined a little in the cold winter months but broke out again with renewed ferocity in the following May. Altogether 259 people perished, out of a total population of 350. One of the victims was Catherine Mompesson, the rector's wife. Out of two leading families, the Talbots and the Hancocks, only one person was left alive when the disease abated at last. There is no doubt that many who died could have saved themselves if they had fled from the village before the plague struck them, but no one did.

Their sacrifice was not in vain. It is true that the hamlet of Foolow, 2 miles away, did suffer an outbreak of plague in October 1665, supposedly caused by a stray dog from Eyam who brought the germs to a farmhouse there. Except for this, the neighbourhood went free.

In the intervening centuries Eyam has prospered and is now one of the largest and most pleasant villages in the Peak District. But once a year, on Wakes Sunday, the last Sunday in August, the villagers' act of collective heroism is recalled in a memorial service for the men and women who died in the epidemic. A long procession of local people and visitors, led by Anglican and Nonconformist clergy and headed by a band, winds its way out to Cucklet Dell. There the service is celebrated as once long ago so many others were, in less happy circumstances. It includes a sermon, prayers and a lesson, and the singing of a special hymn known as 'The Plague Hymn'.

Eyam is 5 miles north of Bakewell, on a side road turning north off the A263 road. In common with a number of Derbyshire towns and villages, there is well-dressing there on the last Saturday in August, and sheep roasting on the green on the first Saturday in September.

Nearest railway stations: Chapel-en-le-Frith, Chesterfield.

FENNY STRATFORD, Buckinghamshire

The Fenny Poppers

In this village, now almost overwhelmed by the new town of Milton Keynes, a ceremony known as Firing the Fenny Poppers takes place every year on Saint Martin's Day (11 November). This is not a traditional Martinmas custom, though it has been observed on that date for some two hundred years. It forms part of the celebrations of the patronal festival of the parish, and it is also a tribute to the memory of Dr Browne Willis, the man who was mainly responsible for the building of the church in 1730.

The Fenny Poppers are six miniature cannon, curiously shaped and believed to be of considerable age, which are normally kept in the belfry of St Martin's Church. On the festival day, they are brought out to the churchyard and solemnly fired, first at 8 a.m., then at noon and at 2.00, and finally at 6.00 p.m. It is customary for the vicar to fire the first Popper.

This odd little ceremony has its roots in the history of the church itself, originally a chapel-of-ease of Bletchley parish. Before the eighteenth century, Fenny Stratford had no church of any kind, and that it has one now is due to the enthusiasm and generosity of Dr Browne Willis, who was patron of the living of Bletchley. He felt that a chapel-of-ease was necessary for Fenny Stratford people and started a subscription for this purpose, contributing generously himself and encouraging the local gentry by selling space on the ceiling of the church for the display of the arms of all those who gave £10 or upwards. These heraldic signs can still be seen stretching from end to end of the ceiling. In 1730 when the church was finished and dedicated to Saint Martin, he arranged for a special sermon to be preached every year on the dedication anniversary, and for a parish feast to be held in the evening. Soon after his death in 1760, the firing of the old cannon which he had presented to the church was added to the other celebrations, and this custom has been kept up ever since.

Fenny Stratford is on the A5 on the outskirts of Bletchley; Woburn Abbey lies about 4 miles to the west.

Nearest railway station: Bletchley.

GRASMERE, Cumbria

Rush-strewing
When the boarding of church floors was still comparatively unusual, rushes were often strewn thickly in the aisles and chapels as a protection against the penetrating cold and damp of stone-flagged or beaten earth floors. This green carpet had to be renewed at least

once a year, usually at the Wakes, when the ceremonial bringing of the new reeds was normally the principal event of the patronal festival. Every part of the parish contributed its quota of sweet-smelling rushes, sometimes carried in bundles by young women dressed in white, but more often piled high on decorated harvest wains, and held in place by flower-decorated ropes and the high harvest-gearing.

The best horses in the village were chosen to draw the carts; Morris dancers usually preceded them, and children and young people walked beside them carrying garlands which were hung in the church after the new rushes had been laid down. Often the procession perambulated the parish in the morning, stopping outside the great houses of the district where the Morris men danced; then, the long round ended, the whole company came to the church, to the sound of pealing bells, and there strewed their rushes on the floor (and sometimes on the graves outside as well), and hung up their garlands in the appointed places. The rest of the day was spent in merrymaking of various kinds.

This custom died out slowly when, with the gradual introduction of wooden church floors, rushes were no longer needed for warmth and dryness. By the 1890s, ceremonial rush-bearing had become fairly rare, but a modified form of it still persists in a number of counties today, particularly in Cumbria. Perhaps the best-known takes place in Grasmere, the Lake District home of Wordsworth, on the Saturday nearest Saint Oswald's Day (5 August). The local people say the ceremony has never lapsed, though before 1885 it was held on the Saturday nearest 20 July. The church floor was boarded in 1841, but the old rush-bearing ceremony continued and is still kept up today.

Here there are rushes in plenty, some carried loose in a hand-woven linen sheet by six young girls, and others carried by villagers in a variety of traditional forms – harps, gates, maypoles, crosses, Saint Oswald's Crown, his wonder-working hand, and many more. They are all carried into the church at the end of a procession round the village and laid along the walls while a service is held. There they are left until the following Monday, when they are fetched away by their owners and another procession sets out for the school field, for sports and tea.

The M5 motorway gives easy access to the Lake District: leave it at junction 36, taking the A591 north-west through Windermere and Ambleside, where there is also rush-bearing (see page 15), by Rydal Water, Grasmere Lake and so to the village itself. Every year, on the Thursday nearest to 20 August, the village also plays host to the famous Grasmere Games, a sort of English Highland Games, with wrestling, fell-racing, hound-trailing and other strenuous contests.

Nearest railway station: Grasmere.

GREAT DUNMOW, Essex

Dunmow Flitch

The Dunmow Flitch is a flitch (or sometimes a gammon) of bacon which has been awarded at intervals during the past six centuries, and possibly for an even longer period, to claimants stating upon oath that having been married for at least a year and a day, they have never once 'sleeping or waking' regret-

ted their marriage or wished themselves single again. This award is still made, though by now what was originally a serious ceremony has degenerated into little more than an hilarious entertainment, usually held on Whit Monday at Great Dunmow in Essex, though sometimes elsewhere.

The medieval home of the custom was Little Dunmow, where a prior of Augustinian canons existed before the Reformation. Exactly when it began is unknown. It is often said to have been instituted by a member of the Fitzwalter family in the thirteenth century, but of this there is no clear proof. The first definite record was made in 1445, but long before that date the custom had been mentioned by William Langland in *The Vision of Piers Plowman* and by Chaucer in the Prologue to *The Wife of Bath's Tale*. Both refer to it quite casually, without explanation, and evidently assume that their readers know all about it.

The applicant was required to go to Little Dunmow Priory and there, kneeling upon two sharp stones, to make the necessary sworn statement in the presence of the prior and the assembled monks and people. 'The Ceremony being long,' says Dugdale in his *Monasticon Anglicanum*, 'it must be painful to him.' Probably it was, but he had his moment of triumph afterwards, when, having won the flitch, he was carried in procession in the prior's chair. This was an ancient wooden stall, with holes under the seat to allow for carrying poles. It is now kept in Little Dunmow Church. Modern applicants are still 'chaired', but today a newer and wider seat is used.

Only three awards are known to have been made before the Reformation, though there may possibly have been others of which we have no record. In 1445 Richard Wright of Bawburgh won the flitch. In 1457 Stephen Samuel of Little Easton received a gammon and in 1510, 'Thomas the fuller of Coggeshall' did likewise. Twenty-six years later, the priory was dissolved, and we hear no more of the Dunmow Flitch for nearly two hundred years.

Nevertheless the manorial obligation to provide the bacon for legitimate claimants still existed, and in 1701 it was honoured at a Court Baron presided over by Thomas Wheeler, steward of the manor of Little Dunmow. A gammon was awarded to John and Anne Reynolds who had lived together in wedded harmony for ten years, and another to William and Jane Parsley, who had done so for three years. This was the first time that the wife was definitely included in the award. Hitherto it had been the husband alone who made the claim and what the wife thought about her married life was not considered. It was also the first recorded time that a jury sat to decide upon the truth of the claims. It consisted of five young women: the steward's daughter and the four daughters of the lord of the manor. In 1751, when Thomas and Ann Shakeshaft received a gammon, six bachelors and six spinsters formed the jury, and this composition has been the customary ever since.

The Flitch ceremony begun in its modern form with the revival of 1885, which was largely due to the enthusiasm of William Harrison Ainsworth, author of *The Tower of London* and many other novels, including *The Flitch of Bacon*, which concerns the attempts of a much-married landlord of the Dunmow inn to win the bacon. This revival took place at Great Dunmow and was a very lively affair, with a splendid procession after the examinations of the claimants in the town hall, followed by sports and other amusements. Now little remains of the custom's former serious character. The trial has become a sort of facetious parody of court proceedings, with a robed and bewigged judge taking the place of the old manor steward, counsel for the claimants and for the bacon, witnesses, court officials and a jury. The applicants have to face a searching cross-examination in a room full of raucous spectators, and those who win the prize certainly deserve to do so, if only for the amusement they provide. Yet in spite of the general atmosphere of merriment, serious claims are still sometimes made, and probably few who were not completely callous and insensitive would care to come forward if their married lives were not in fact peaceful and happy.

This merry village may be found on the A120, about 9 miles to the east of Bishop's Stortford.

Nearest railway station: Bishop's Stortford.

GREAT WISHFORD, Wiltshire

Grovely

Great Wishford, or Wishford Magna, lies some 6 miles to the north-west of Salisbury, and here a custom connected with the maintenance of wood-gathering rights in Grovely Forest is annually practised on 29 May. Although the Wishford celebrations have now been held on Oak Apple Day for a very long time, they have no real connection with that festival except in so far as they appear to have been transferred to it from their original Whitsun-tide date as an expression of loyalty. The forest privileges which are preserved by the observance of the Grovely custom are far older than the Restoration and were described in a document drawn up in 1603 as having existed 'ever by auntient custome and tyme out of mind'.

This document, sometimes referred to as the 'Book of Rights', is a record of the proceedings of a Court held in Grovely Forest on 15 March 1603. It sets forth all the 'olde auntient and laudable customes' then enjoyed by the manors of Wishford and Barford St Martin, and is signed by ten local men, one of whom bears the curious name of Catkat. Some of the privileges listed therein have now disappeared or have been exchanged for fiscal payments by various owners of the woodlands, but the right to gather 'all kinde of deade snappinge wood Boughes and Stickes' for firewood still remains. Such wood can be gathered at any time and once a year (now on Oak Apple Day), green boughs are cut and brought in. These boughs have to be 'drawen by strength of people', without mechanical aids. Handcarts may be used, but horse-drawn carts are not allowed nor, of course, is any form of motor transport. When bicycles were invented there was some debate about them, but finally it was decided that since human strength is necessary to move them, their use could be permitted.

The modern Grovely ceremonies begin at about 3.00 a.m, when the local young men march through the village with drums and bugles, shouting 'Grovely, Grovely, and all Grovely!' They stop outside the houses to greet and be greeted by those whom they have awakened by their noisy passage. They go to Grovely Woods and there they cut their green branches, some of which are set before the doors of houses in the village, while others are carried in a grand procession held later in the day. Practically every house and cottage sports its oak bough on this anniversary, and every man, woman and child wears a sprig of oak leaves or oak apples. One large branch known as the Marriage Bough is decorated with ribbons and hauled to the top of the church tower, there to bring good luck to all who are married in the church during the following year.

One of the most interesting ceremonies of this crowded day is the visit to Salisbury Cathedral. In the 1603 'Book of Rights' it is recorded that

> the lords, freeholders, Tennants and Inhabitance of the Mannor of greate Wishford . . . have used to goe in a daunce to the Cathedrall Church of our blessed Ladie in the Cittie of newe Sarum on Whit Tuesdaie in the said Countie of Wiltes, and theire made theire clayme to theire custome in the Forrest of Groveley in theis wordes; Grovely Grovely and all Grovely.

It is said that formerly those taking part in this ritual, dressed all in white and carrying oak branches, danced along the whole six miles between the village and the city. On arrival, they first danced before the cathedral and then, entering and standing before the high altar, made public claim to their rights by shouting the historic words. This custom continued until the beginning of the nineteenth century, by which time a kind of unofficial fair had grown up round it. Stalls and booths were erected in the Close, and a general revel took place. Eventually this became offensive to the cathedral authorities and was suppressed. The dancing and claim-shouting was then transferred to the village and was enacted in front of the rectory.

For some years it was customary for two women, representing the bough-gatherers, to go alone to Salisbury and reverently lay oak-sprigs before the altar, but in time even this ceased. In 1951, however, this ancient and important part of the Grovely ceremonies was revived, and now, during the morning of Oak Apple Day, four women, carrying sprigs from an oak tree and accompanied by numerous villagers, travel to the city, where they dance upon the cathedral green. This being done, the whole company goes into the cathedral to make their claim in the traditional form by standing before the altar and crying 'Grovely! Grovely! and All Grovely!' Afterwards all return to Wishford to take part in the remaining celebrations of the day.

A procession is formed at the Town-End Tree at the south end of the village. In it walk the same four women who danced at Salisbury, now carrying faggots of snapwood on their heads, schoolchildren carrying flowers and led by their May Queen and the people of the village carrying oak boughs and a banner. The handcarts used for gathering wood in the forest also appear, now decorated in various ways. After the procession has marched around the village, there is a ceremonial lunch in a marquee. The rest of the day is spent in a variety of amusements cheerfully enjoyed in the knowledge that the privileges of the community have been safely preserved for another year.

Nearest railway station: Salisbury.

GUILDFORD, Surrey

Maids' Money

In 1674, John How, of Guildford, left £400 for the benefit of a charity since known as Maids' Money. The interest was to be diced for by two maids who had qualified, according to his terms, by remaining in service in the same Guildford household for two clear years, provided only that the house in question was neither an inn nor an alehouse.

The full amount was to go to the girl who threw the highest number; there was no provision for a second prize. These days, however, there is one. In 1702 John Parsons, another Guildford man, left £600 with directions that the interest should go to some poor young man at the end of his seven-year apprenticeship who was willing to swear before a magistrate that, at that time, he was not worth £20. Should no young man present himself in any one year, the money was to go to a maid-servant 'of good repute' who had served in a private house for three consecutive years. In the course of time, applications from apprentices failed, and the bequest became permanently attached to John How's Maids' Money. The girl who comes second in the dicing competition receives John Parson's award, with the rather singular result that, as his original gift was greater than that of How, the loser gains rather more than the winner.

The competition takes place every year in January, in the Guild Hall.

Nearest railway station: Guildford.

GUISELEY, West Yorkshire

Clipping the Church

An ancient 'clipping the church' ceremony takes place on 5 August, Saint Oswald's Day, at Guiseley. Saint Oswald is the patron saint of the parish church and the parishioners walk around the church in procession as a symbolic gesture of their love for it.

'Clipping' is an old English word for encircling. For more about the possible origins of the ritual, see *Painswick*, page 70.

Guiseley lies between Bradford and Leeds, 2 or 3 miles to the north and just off the A65.

Nearest railway station: Leeds.

HALLATON, Leicestershire

Scrambling and Bottle-kicking

The Hare Pie Scramble, which still takes place on Easter Monday in the village of Hallaton, is probably of medieval origin, though no one knows now when it actually began. It is followed immediately by a strenuous inter-parish game known as Bottle-kicking, which may well be very much older. The Scramble is connected with a piece of land which, at some date now unknown, was settled upon the successive rectors of the parish, on condition that each in his turn provided every

Easter two hare pies, a quantity of ale, and two dozen penny loaves, to be scrambled for on the rising ground known as Hare Pie Bank.

The special mention of hares for the pies at a time when they are out of season suggests that this bequest may have absorbed some older custom associated with the ancient concept of the Easter Hare – the hare was the sacred beast of Eastre (or Eostre), a Saxon goddess of spring and of the dawn from whose name the English word 'Easter' may have been derived. In this connection it is interesting to note that in some years a figure of a sitting hare mounted upon a pole has been carried in the procession to the bank. It is hardly necessary to say that the modern pies (now more usually one very large pie in place of the original two) do not contain hare but are made of beef, or some other meat.

They are cut up by the rector, and the resulting small pieces are then put into a sack and ceremonially carried to Hare Pie Bank. A long procession winds round the village, and in it march three men carrying the so-called bottles that will be used in the game. These bottles are in fact small wooden barrels,

strongly made and hooped with iron. Two contain ale, the third is a dummy. During the parade they are held high in the air, balanced upon the flat of the bearer's hand. When the procession reaches the bank, the sack is emptied and the pieces of pie are scrambled for by the waiting crowd with as much energy and excitement as might be shown if Easter Monday dinner depended upon them. Formerly the loaves were scrambled for also, but these have now vanished from the proceedings, an equivalent and perhaps more useful gift for the aged poor of the village having been substituted for them at the end of last century.

After the Scramble is finished, the Bottle-kicking begins. One of the full barrels is thrown into a circular hollow on top of the bank. A vigorous contest then follows between two teams of players, the men of Hallaton on one side and the Medbourne side on the other. Medbourne is the adjoining parish but the team bearing its name does not necessarily consist only of its inhabitants. It may include 'strangers' from another village or, indeed, anyone who is not a Hallatonian. There is no limit on numbers, and as many as will can play on either side. Several hundred participants may be an underestimate of the total squad for the match.

The object of the game is to get the bottle away from the bank and over the boundary in one direction or the other. Whichever team succeeds in kicking it over their own line has won that round and can claim the contents of the barrel. Much fierce struggling is needed before this can be achieved, the competition for possession of the bottle often resembling a massive rugger scrum, and the contest usually lasts for a considerable time. When it is over, the dummy bottle is fought for with even greater vigour and enthusiasm. Finally, the second full barrel is carried in triumph at the game's end to the old Market Cross on Hallaton Green, where it is broached with full honours and its contents are shared by both sides. The leader of the winning team is hoisted onto the top of the cross and in that rather uncomfortable position he takes the first drink. The barrels used in this boisterous game are carefully kept from year to year, repainted and decorated for each occasion, and only replaced when they have become too battered to be of further service.

From time to time, attempts have been made to suppress both parts of this cheerful celebration, usually on the grounds that the Bottle-kicking is too rowdy and the money needed for the Hare Pie Scramble might be better employed. One rector in the eighteenth century tried to divert the funds to other charitable uses, but he met with so much opposition that he had to abandon the idea. 'No pie, no parson, and a job for the glazier!' was chalked all over the rectory doors and walls and on the outside of the church. In 1878 when the railway was being built and Hallaton was feeling 'modern', it was proposed to substitute other and quieter sports for the wild Bottle-kicking. But this proposal failed like the other and today, notwithstanding two world wars and some local difficulties, Hallaton's annual Easter Monday festival still preserves its ancient two-part form and is celebrated with as much vigour as in the past.

Hallaton, called Alctone in the Domesday Book, is 7 miles to the north-east of Market Harborough in the lush grazing lands of the Welland Valley. It is best approached from the village of Norton, on the A47 road between Leicester and Uppingham. Turn south on a by-road at Norton, and Hallaton is about 2 miles distant.

Nearest railway station: Market Harborough.

HAXEY, Lincolnshire

The Hood Game

The old and unusual game known as the Hood Game, or Throwing the Hood, is played every year on Old Christmas Day, 6 January, at Haxey. On this date, Haxey Hood, one of the two annual feasts of the parish, is held. The other, Haxey Midsummer, falls on or near 6 July and is much like other village feasts elsewhere, but Haxey Hood has a character all its own. It is the great festive occasion of the parish year, when everyone keeps holiday and some very interesting traditional customs are observed.

The ceremonies of Haxey Hood begin in the early afternoon with the procession of the Fool and his twelve Boggans up the village street to a small green outside the parish church. The Boggans are the official team of players in the Hood Game and play against all comers; they are, and need to be, vigorous young men, who are often useful members of the local football team. Chief among them is the King Boggan, or Lord of the Hood, who carries a wand, or roll, of thirteen willows bound with thirteen withy-bands as a badge of office. Tradition demands that he and all his team should wear scarlet flannel coats and hats wreathed with red flowers. The Lord usually does so, though his coat is not always made of

flannel now. So do some of his men, but quite often a red jersey or shirt replaces the coat. Invariably the ritual red appears somewhere on the Boggans' dress, if only in the form of an armband or some fluttering scarlet ribbons.

The Fool, who leads the procession and has the right to kiss any woman he chooses throughout the day, also has a good deal of red about him. His face is smeared with soot and red ochre, and his sackcloth trousers are patched with pieces of red cloth cut in a variety of shapes. His shirt, or coat, is red and so are the flowers that adorn his fine feathered hat. He carries a whip with a sock filled with bran at the end of the thong, and this he uses for the time-honoured purpose of belabouring those unwary enough to come within reach.

During the week before Old Christmas Day, the Fool and the Boggans go round the nearby villages, singing 'John Barleycorn', 'The Farmer's Boy' and 'Drink England Dry', and inviting all and sundry to come to the hood-throwing. At the same time they collect money for the festival expenses. All wear full ceremonial attire, although the Fool's face is not smeared. On the day itself, when the procession reaches the green by the churchyard, the Fool mounts upon a stone which once formed the base of a tall cross. There he makes a traditional speech welcoming all present and inviting them to join in the game, and mysteriously stating that two bullocks and a half have been killed but the other half had to be left running about the field, and can be fetched if wanted. Finally he reminds his hearers that the order of the day is:

Hoose agen hoose,
Toon agen toon,
If tho' meets a man, knock 'im doon,
But don't 'ut 'im!

While he is speaking, a small fire of damp straw is lit behind him, and a cloud of smoke billows around. This is known as Smoking the Fool and is a modern version of an ancient ceremony which formerly took place on the morning after the Hood Game. Some straw was set alight under a tree and the Fool was tied to a branch above it. Suspended over the fire, he was swung backwards and forwards until almost suffocated; then he was allowed to drop into the smouldering straw, which was well wetted, and scramble out as best he could. This custom, with its suggestions of ritual fumigation, had counterparts elsewhere; it persisted in the Haxey area until almost within living memory but eventually it was abandoned because of its obvious dangers. Before the Second World War the modern form of the custom seems to have been practised only intermittently, but of recent years it has become a usual part of the festivities. It is certainly safer than the old way, but even so it has its perils. In 1956 someone forgot to damp the straw and the Fool caught fire. However, many willing hands soon extinguished the blaze.

As soon as the speechmaking and Smoking are over, the Fool leads the way up the hill to a half-acre of ground near the top. Here the game begins. The Boggans stand in a wide circle and the Lord of the Hood and players from Haxey, Westwoodside, and the other parts of the wide parish stand inside the ring so made. The Lord throws up the first hood, one of several minor hoods which are played for first. These hoods bear no resemblance to headgear; the lesser ones are tightly rolled pieces of canvas tied with ribbons, and the main, or Leather Hood, which is played for later in the game, is a two-foot length of thick rope encased in stout leather. As soon as the first hood is thrown up, there is a fierce struggle, every man trying to seize it and carry it over the boundary to his own village. If anyone manages to get it safely over the line and away, he can keep the hood; but in order to do so he has to elude not only the watchful Boggans but all the other players, who rush after him and try to wrest it from him. The function of the Boggans is to prevent the hood from crossing the boundary. If one of them captures it, or even touches it, that hood is 'dead' and is returned to the Lord to be thrown up again.

When all the minor hoods have been disposed of, the Sway, the really serious part of the game, begins. The Leather or Sway Hood is produced and is thrown straight up into the air, either by the Lord or by some prominent person present who has been invited to do so as a mark of honour. The ring of Boggans breaks up, and all semblance of orderly play disappears. Somebody seizes the hood, but he does not run away with it because rapid independent movement has instantly become impossible.

A solid compact mass of struggling humanity pours slowly down the hill, swaying backwards and forwards as the varying pressure of the pushing, heaving crowd dictates. The hood may not be kicked or tossed forward but only 'swayed', that is, pushed, pulled, or dragged towards one of the three inns which serve as the 'goals' of this energetic contest.

Every local man who is not too old is expected to take part in the grimly earnest struggle. Stragglers are rounded up by the Boggans and men on the edge of the watching crowds may be swept into the Sway as it moves slowly onwards. Everything in its path goes down before it, including hedges and sometimes even stone walls. Two hours or more go by before one faction or another is finally victorious, but at long last the contest does end and the Sway Hood is brought in triumph to the winners' inn. The landlord provides free drinks for all and the hood remains in his keeping until next Haxey Hood, except when it is needed for some reason and is fetched away by the Fool or the Boggans then in office. At one time, it used to be ceremonially roasted before the inn fire and doused with ale as it turned on the spit, the ale being then drunk by those present, but of this interesting aspect of the ritual no trace now remains.

Like many other ancient rites whose origins have been forgotten, the Hood Game is explained locally by a legend. This says that in the thirteenth century Lady Mowbray, then lady of the manor, lost her scarlet hood in a high wind when she was riding from Haxey to Westwoodside. The flying hood was pursued and caught by twelve labourers who happened to be working nearby, though not without con-siderable difficulty because of the strength of the wind. As a reward for their help, she bestowed upon the parish thirteen half-acres of land, the rent of which was to provide a feast and a hood to be played for every year on the same day forever. This tale is supposed to account for the number of the Boggans, their important duties in the ceremonies and the red clothes that they wear. The piece of ground on which the Hood Game always begins is said to be the place where her hood blew off; presumably it is also one of the half-acres that she gave. Exactly where the other twelve were is now unknown, for the deeds have all been lost.

It seems very likely, however, that the roots of the custom run much farther back in time than the thirteenth century, and that what has now become a game and a feast began as a pre-Christian fertility rite associated with the end of the midwinter festival and the beginning of spring. The ferocity of the struggle for possession of the Leather Hood, the fact that the captured Hood was once roasted by the victors, the Smoking of the Fool and the reference to bullocks in his speech, all point to such a beginning.

A form of Hood Game is also played at Epworth, close to Haxey, but the custom is not so regularly observed and the method of play is somewhat different. Haxey people allege that the Epworth Hood is merely an imitation of their own game.

Haxey lies 5 miles south of the M18 motorway between Doncaster and Scunthorpe. Turn south at junction 2, taking the A161 through Belton, Epworth and Low Bursham.

Nearest railway station: Doncaster.

HELSTON, Cornwall

The Furry Dance

The Furry Dance at Helston is one of the most interesting, and probably one of the oldest examples of the communal spring festival dance still surviving in Great Britain. It has been performed in Helston for centuries, according to the local people, without a break, except in times of war and pestilence. At one time, similar dances took place at the Lizard on 1 May and at Penrhyn on 3 May, but these have vanished, while the Helston custom is as fresh and vigorous today as ever it was in the past.

Furry Day falls on 8 May, the Feast of the Apparition of Saint Michael the Archangel, who is the patron saint of the parish. Various local legends are told to explain its ceremonies. One is that Saint Michael and the Devil fought for the possession of the town, and that the people danced in the streets for joy when the battle was won by the archangel. Another says that the fight took place at Mont St Michel in Brittany and that the result was somewhat less definite. Saint Michael was forced to take refuge on St Michael's Mount, near Marazion, but fortunately Satan feared to cross the sea and contented himself with removing the great stone that sealed the mouth of Hell and throwing it after his enemy. It fell short by nine miles and landed in the yard of the Angel Hotel in Helston. So huge a block of granite might have done immense damage, but Saint Michael protected his people, and no one was hurt. On that day, then, they danced, as they have done on the anniversary ever since; in proof of the legend, the stone, or part of it, may still be seen, built into the west wall of the hotel.

In the course of centuries, the festival has been variously called Flora, Faddy, or Furry Day, the last being now the most usual name; it is probably derived from the Cornish *feur*, a fair or jubilee. Today as in the past it is the great holiday of the town's year. For two or three weeks beforehand, everyone is busy painting, whitewashing and generally smartening up the houses and gardens. On 1 May there is a sort of preliminary canter. The town band parades through the streets at 6.00 a.m. and 7.00 p.m. playing the Furry Dance music. It is followed by hundreds of dancing children whose performance, unlike that of a week later, is entirely spontaneous and not in any way organized.

On the great day itself, houses and public buildings are decorated with branches of sycamore and beech, flowers and evergreens. The church bells are pealed and a special early morning service is held in St Michael's Church. At seven o'clock the Early Morning Dance, the first of the day, begins. This is for the young people who, like their elders later on, dance in a traditional fashion through the narrow streets and in and out of gardens and houses, all of them wearing lilies-

of-the-valley, the particular flower of the festival. While this is going on, other young people are out in the woods gathering yet more green branches. With these they walk round the town accompanied by young men dressed as Saint Michael and Saint George, Robin Hood, Friar Tuck and Little John. At certain points fixed by tradition, they stop to sing the ancient Hal-an-Tow song, one verse of which shows very clearly what it is that they are all celebrating. It runs:

> With Hal-an-Tow! Jolly Rumble, O!
> For we are up as soon as any day, O,
> And for to fetch the Summer home,
> The Summer and the May, O,
> For Summer is a-come, O,
> And Winter is a-gone, O.

At 10 a.m. the children dance, all in white and wearing the traditional lilies. Each school sends a contingent. Then, exactly at noon, the principal dance begins. The mayor goes first, wearing his chain of office, and behind him come men and women in couples, the men in morning coats and top hats, and the women in their prettiest summer frocks. They dance through all the main streets and into gardens, shops and houses, in at one door and, if possible, out through another, to bring the luck of summer to the owners and tenants and drive out the darkness of winter.

The last dance begins at five o'clock, led by the young people who danced first. The spectators may join in, and most of them do, so that at the end of the day the whole town seems to be dancing.

What is really remarkable about Helston's Furry Day is its essentially unchanging character. In spite of the thousands of visitors who come to see it, it has never been commercialized or used to raise money for charity. It remains a communal festival, a celebration in which everyone, from the mayor down to the youngest schoolchild, takes part. The ancient origins of the festival show clearly in the green boughs gathered so early and carried about; in the words of the traditional song; and in the never-omitted luckbringing visits. If any pre-Christian ancestor of today's dancers could return on Furry Day now, he would probably have little difficulty in recognizing the traces of those rites by which he too once brought the summer home and carried luck and fertility into every house.

Nearest railway station: Redruth.

HINTON ST GEORGE, Somerset

Punkie Night

The last Thursday in October is Punkie Night in this ancient village a little to the north of Crewkerne. On this night a little festival of lights is held, for which the children make punkies, or candle lanterns, from hollowed-out mangold-wurzels. These are similar in form to the lanterns made elsewhere for Halloween, but they are more elaborate. Instead of the simple holes for eyes and nose of the usual Hallowtide face, quite intricate flower, ship or animal patterns are cut on the outer skin of the mangold. The inner pith is removed, except for the small amount needed to preserve the lantern shape, and a short piece of candle is set inside. When the candle is lit the result is a most effective and pleasing lantern, shedding a soft, glowing light. The finished punkies are carried on strings threaded through two holes near the top. With them the children parade the streets for about two hours in the evening, visiting the houses and singing:

> It's Punkie Night tonight.
> Give us a candle, give us a light,
> If you don't, you'll get a fright.

> It's Punkie Night tonight.
> Adam and Eve, they'd never believe
> It's Punkie Night tonight.

It is usual for the children to go round beforehand to beg the necessary candles from local householders. It is, or was, considered very unlucky to refuse to give. Shortly before the outbreak of the Second World War, a newly appointed constable, coming from another area and unfamiliar with the custom, tried to stop the parades. This action on the part of a 'foreigner' was hotly resented by the villagers. A complaint was made to the Chief Constable in Taunton, by whose orders the ban was lifted. Since then the celebration has gone on without further disturbance.

Local tradition says that Punkie Night was once connected with the now extinct Chiselborough Fair, though no one seems to know exactly what the connection was. In fact the Punkie Night custom, regardless of its date, really belongs to the Hallowtide Guisers' ritual, in which the strange lanterns and their bearers represented the returning dead. It is kept up in some other south Somerset villages also, where the punkies are carried about not on a fixed day as at Hinton St George, but during the week in which Halloween falls.

Nearest railway station: Crewkerne.

HUNGERFORD, Berkshire

Hocktide Festival
The Monday and Tuesday after Low Sunday (the first Sunday after Easter) are together known as Hocktide. This short festival is now almost forgotten, but until the middle of the seventeenth century it was an occasion for sports and games, and for the collection of money for church and parish expenses. Hock Tuesday was also a recognized day for the payment of rents in districts where the year was divided for land-tenure purposes into two halves beginning at Hocktide and at Michaelmas.

Only at Hungerford is Hocktide still observed as a festival, but since it is also, and indeed primarily, an important civic occasion there, the celebrations are not quite the same as those once found in other places. Unlike most English boroughs, Hungerford has no mayor or corporation, although some-one has the courtesy title, Chairman of the Town Council. Instead, it has a Constable and ten Trustees (or Feoffees) chosen from the commoners of the town, a High Constable, Bailiff, Port-reeve, Tutti-men, and other officials. These officers are elected for the ensuing year at the Hocktide Court which, according to a document in the borough archives, 'is and time out of mind always hath been kept and holden on the Tuesday called Hockney-day'. The actual election is in the hands of twelve persons but, in theory at least, all the commoners are bound to attend the court and also the Court Baron on the following Friday when the newly elected officials are sworn in.

The Tuesday Court now meets at 9.00 a.m. Formerly it met at 8.00, and at that hour still the Town Crier appears on the Town Hall balcony and blows a long blast upon a bugle-horn. This horn is a replica, made in 1634, of one far older which John of Gaunt gave to the townspeople in 1364, when he also bestowed upon them certain manorial privileges, including the right of free fishery, three days a week, in the River Kennet. The privileges and the horn still exist, but the latter is no longer sounded on Hock Day. Instead the 'new' horn is used to open the proceedings as it has been since it was first made. It bears the date 1634 and an inscription stating:

JOHN A GAUN DID GIVE AND GRANT THE RIALL
OF FISHING TO HUNGERFORD TOUNE FROM
ELDRED STUB TO IRISH STILL EXCEPTING SOM
SEURAL MILL POUND
JEHOSOPHAT LUCAS WAS CUNSTABL

While the court is sitting to elect its officers and deal with other manorial concerns, two Tutti-men, or Tything-men, set out on their rounds accompanied by an individual known as the Orange Scrambler, who carries a sack of oranges and wears cock's feathers round his top hat. The Tything-men were originally officials whose duty during their year of office was to keep watch and ward over the inhabitants and their property.

They go first to the Town Hall to receive their tutti-poles. These are two long staves adorned with ribbons and a 'tutti', or posy of flowers, and surmounted by an orange. Armed with these, they visit every common-right house in the town to collect their dues, traditionally a 'headpenny', a penny from each person. Women have the right to pay with a kiss if they so wish and this has by now become the more usual procedure. For each kiss, an orange is given, taken from the top of the tutti-pole, and every child in the house receives one as well. As each orange is removed from the pole, it is replaced by another from the Orange Scrambler's sack. The Tutti-men are also entitled to stop any woman they meet in the streets, whether she be resident, visitor or simply passing motorist, and to demand from her the same payment of a penny or a kiss.

At the end of their morning round, they go to the Three Swans Hotel, where a civic luncheon is held for Feoffees, officials and local notables. Here the newly elected Constable presides, and on either side of the chair the tutti-poles are set up. When the meal is over the Tutti-men and the Orange Scrambler go outside and scatter oranges and pennies to a joyous crowd of waiting children. Meanwhile inside the hotel the ceremony of Shoeing the Colt takes place. The guests at the luncheon normally include a certain number of newcomers to the town and so, when the toasts have been drunk, the Constable rises to announce that there are 'strangers present' and that the colt must be shod. Two men then enter, one carrying a hammer and the other bearing a box of farrier's nails. Each 'colt' or stranger is seized in turn by the pair, who drive a nail into the heel of his shoe until he cries 'Punch!' and pays for his release with a further bowl of punch. Thus he ceases to be a stranger and is admitted to the company of Hungerford men.

To witness the public portions of the ceremony at least, and to visit the handsome old town itself, you should take exit 14 from the M4 motorway; the A338 leads from there directly into Hungerford.

Nearest railway station: Hungerford.

IDEFORD, Devon

Easter Charity

In 1585 Bartholomew Borrington of

Ideford charged certain lands with an annual payment of £1 which, in the form of twenty new shillings, was to be laid upon his tomb every Maundy Thursday and given to twenty poor people of the parish. This is still done, although in the course of time the day has been changed to Good Friday. The rector and the churchwardens stand at one end of the tomb in the churchyard and lay the coins upon its flat top; the beneficiaries come one by one to the opposite end and pick up their money.

Ideford is a village on the A380, and is situated 2 miles north of Newton Abbott.

Nearest railway station: Newton Abbott.

JERSEY

Battle of the Flowers

Just eighty years ago, in 1902, the Channel island of Jersey organized a magnificent flower festival in celebration of the coronation of King Edward VII and Queen Alexandra. It proved such a resounding success that the islanders resolved to hold one annually. Its popularity has grown steadily over the decades until it is now Europe's greatest floral carnival, attracting many thousands of holidaymakers who converge on the island's capital, St Helier, for the event.

What has come to be known as the Battle of the Flowers usually takes place during the fourth week of July. Millions of blooms are cultivated specially for the occasion and are used to decorate floats, lorries, cars and wagons, which form a grand parade. The island's beauty queen, Miss Jersey, rides on a splendid throne of blossoms; episodes from history are depicted in exotic floral tableaux, along with dozens of ingeniously constructed novelties ranging from peacocks and elephants to windmills and aeroplanes.

The climax of the festivities comes when, at a given signal, a great battle of flowers commences, with exhibitors and spectators bombarding each other with blooms. However, the battle is of the friendliest nature imaginable, great care being taken that the flowers used are devoid of hard stems and thorns; there is also a rule that the floats and other exhibits must not be stripped and used as 'ammunition'.

Jersey is accessible by frequent ferry and airline services.

KIDDERMINSTER, Worcestershire

Peace and Good Neighbourhood Dinner

About five hundred years ago an unmarried woman, whose name is now forgotten, left forty shillings to the inhabitants of Church Street, Kidderminster, in order to provide, every year on Midsummer Eve, a farthing loaf for each child born in that street or living in it. She also expressed a wish that the person acting as trustree for this money should, on the same day, invite to his house all the men of the street, so that they might meet together in friendship, and settle any differences that might have arisen between any of them in the year just passed. Because of the bequest, the anniversary was long known in the neighbourhood as Farthing Loaf Day.

The money was lost for a time, owing to a bad investment, but kindly local individuals replaced it and in 1776 it was supplemented by the will of John Brecknell, himself a resident of Church

Street. He left £150 to pay for a twopenny plum cake to be given to every child or unmarried woman in the street, in addition to the farthing loaves already provided, and also for pipes, tobacco and ale for the men who attended the Midsummer meeting. This latter gift was, he says in his will, given to foster 'the better establishment and continuance of the said Friendly Meeting for Ever'. Any remaining money was to be given to the poor in sums of not more than five or less than two shillings for each person.

These two bequests were the foundation of the Peace and Good Neighbourhood Dinner, now held every year at mid-summer. The chairman asks at the beginning if anyone in Church Street is at odds with his neighbour, and offers to try to reconcile them if that is the case. The main toast at the dinner is 'Peace and Good Neighbourhood', and these words are also said when the cakes and loaves, and the money gifts to the poor, are distributed to the people of Church Street.

The thriving town of Kidderminster, famous for its carpets, is a few miles to the south-west of Birmingham, midway between Worcester and Wolverhampton on the A449 road.

Nearest railway station: Kidderminster.

KINGS CAPLE, Herefordshire

Pax Cakes

The distribution of Pax Cakes on Palm Sunday at Sellack and Kings Caple is a ceremony which certainly dates from the sixteenth century, and may be far older. In about 1570, Lady Scudamore, a local landowner, charged the revenues of Baysham Court with three annual payments of 5s. 9d. each to provide cake and ale every year on Palm Sunday for the parishioners of the neighbouring villages. Of this money, five shillings was to pay for the cake and the odd ninepence was to be spent on ale. The food and drink were to be given at the morning service and consumed in the church.

The donor believed that in this way peace and friendship at the holy season of Easter would be ensured, since those who had shared a common meal in church would surely be readier to compose any quarrels that might exist between them and to come together in amity to their Easter Communion a week later. Although there is no doubt that Lady Scudamore's benefaction was inspired by this pious intention, it is by no means certain that the custom itself was new in her day. It has a strong pre-Reformation flavour about it, and it is quite probable that, as with some other endowed customs, her money was given to preserve an ancient ritual that was already in existence rather than to inaugurate something quite new.

One large cake was provided and presented by the churchwardens to the vicar, who cut the first slice. The rest was then carried round to the people in their seats. At one time it seems to have been usual for the clergyman to break his cake with some of his principal parishioners, and for others in the congregation to break theirs with their neighbours, saying 'Peace and good neighbourhood' or 'Peace and good will' as they did so. Glasses of ale were also distributed, but at some time in the nineteenth century the funds to pay for this were lost, perhaps because of the falling value of the bequest money. For some years thereafter the deficiency was supplied by local farmers who brought their own ale or cider to the service; eventually, with changing ideas of decorum, this ceased and only the cake remained.

Later the single large cake was replaced by small cakes, one for each person. An account written in 1907 tells of baskets covered by a white cloth, and filled with buns, being carried round by the churchwardens immediately after the collection. The writer adds that these cakes 'well within living memory of the inhabitants of Sellack . . . have been the means of settling bitter feuds, notably between two sisters just before one of them passed away'.

Nowadays the Pax Cakes are small flat wafers stamped with the image of the Paschal Lamb. They are no longer distributed or eaten in the church, but are handed by the vicar, standing outside the church door, to everyone as they come out of the building. As he does this, the clergyman says 'God and Good Neighbourhood' to every recipient, as a reminder of the intention of this ancient ceremony.

The village of Kings Caple is 10 miles or so south of Hereford, along a meandering side road that runs east off the A49 between Llandinabo and The Cleaver. Drive into Hoarwithy, then fork right for Kings Caple. Sellack is just south, across the River Wye.

Nearest railway station: Hereford.

KINGSTEIGNTON, Devon

Ram Roasting Fair

This ceremony takes place annually on Whit Monday. The decorated carcase of a ram lamb is carried in procession through the streets, and is afterwards roasted on a spit before a great open-air fire by the side of Oakford Lawn. The roasting takes about four hours, during which time sports and maypole dancing take place. Then the cooked meat is cut up and slices are distributed to the spectators.

This celebration is a modified form of a custom which formerly extended over the Monday and Tuesday of Whit Week. On the Monday, a living lamb was adorned with flowers and ribbons and drawn through the village in a garlanded and canopied cart, a sacrificial victim due to die for the good of the people on the following day. On the Tuesday it was killed and the dressed and decorated carcase was paraded on a handbarrow before being roasted and carved up for distribution.

A description of the ceremony as it was until about 1883 states that the slices were sold for a penny or threepence, and that the sports took place on the high road. At about this time the procession of the living lamb was abandoned, though the carcase was still carried through the village on the Tuesday. For many years, the celebrations were confined to Whit Tuesday, but later they were transferred to the Monday to give bank-holiday revellers a chance to take part. During most of the Second World War the Ram Roasting Fair was in abeyance but in 1946 it began again. Meat rationing was still in force, but undaunted the Kingsteington people roasted various substitute animals, the most usual being a deer presented by Lord Clifford of Chudleigh, or by the Earl of Devon. In 1952 when no deer was available, a reindeer was procured from London.

Legend connects the origin of the custom with a dearth of water. Until piped water came to the village in 1895, the main source of supply was the Fairwater, a stream which runs through the churchyard and is said never to run dry, even in the hottest weather. Tradition has it that it did so once, on some undated occasion in the pre-Christian past, and that the people sacrificed a ram in the dry bed of the leat. As soon as they had done so, the water flowed again; thereafter the same offering was made evey year, in thanksgiving, according to some accounts, but more probably to ensure that the failure of the stream should never be repeated.

Kingsteignton is on the A381, about 1 mile north of Newton Abbott.

Nearest railway station: Newton Abbott.

KNIGHTLOW CROSS,
Warwickshire

Wroth Silver

Wroth Silver is money annually due from various parishes of Knightlow Hundred to the Duke of Buccleuch, who is lord of that hundred. Very strict and obviously ancient rules govern its collection. It has to be paid before sunrise on Saint Martin's Day, 11 November, at Knightlow Cross, which stands in a roadside field not far from Dunchurch. Here the representatives of the parishes concerned meet to hear the Duke's agent read the 'Charter of Assembly' and, as he calls upon them severally to do so, to drop their coins into a hollow in the large stone which is all that now remains of the cross. Each man as he makes his payment says, 'Wroth Silver'. Formerly, as Sir William Dugdale records in his *Antiquities of Warwickshire*, each man was also required to walk round the stone three times before laying his money in the hollow. The sums due vary from one penny to 16p. When all the payments have been made the entire company, led by the agent, goes to the Dun Cow Inn at Stretton-on-Dunsmore, where they have breakfast at the Duke's expense and drink his health in rum and milk.

The payment of Wroth Silver is a very old custom which is said to run back to Anglo-Saxon times. It has been variously explained as money originally given for exemption from military service, or as a form of wayleave-payment to secure the right to drive cattle over Dunsmore Heath. The total sum collected each year does not exceed 50p, which certainly cannot cover the cost of the breakfast given by the Duke after the ceremony. Nevertheless, payment is rigidly enforced and the penalties for default are not of a kind to encourage evasion. For every penny left unpaid, a fine of £1 or, alternatively, of a white bull with red ears and a red nose can be imposed. Such an animal would be exceedingly difficult to find today, and probably has been for a very long time, for the description suggests the old wild cattle of England which are now virtually extinct. The fine in this form was imposed at least once during the eighteenth century, 'a white bull having been demanded by the Steward of the late Lord John Scott, then Lord of the Hundred'.

Stretton-on-Dunsmore is just south of the A45, some 5 miles east of Coventry.

Nearest railway station: Coventry.

LEWES, Sussex

Bonfire Night

By the arrest of Guy Fawkes on 5 November 1605 the failure of the

Gunpowder Plot was assured. A thankful Parliament ordered that the day should henceforth be observed as a holiday with general rejoicings, the pealing of bells, the firing of cannon and a special service to be held in all churches. A wave of anti-Catholic feeling swept the country especially in those areas where, for one reason or another, it was already very strong, and in such places faint traces of ancient hatreds still linger on into the modern Bonfire Night celebrations. At Lewes, where seventeen Protestants were burned as heretics on School Hill during the reign of Mary I, an eighteenth-century 'No Popery' banner is often carried in the processions; until very recently, an effigy of the Pope was burnt along with that of Guy Fawkes.

Lewes still celebrates 5 November with the biggest bonfires and longest torchlight processions in Britain. The proceedings begin with the marching of each of the six bonfire societies in turn to the war memorial where wreaths are laid, hymns are sung and there is a short sermon in which England's deliverance long ago is remembered. There are then elaborate bonfire ceremonies, fireworks and splendid torchlight processions that wind through the town until nearly midnight, when they converge on the bridge and a blazing tar barrel is hurled into the River Ouse.

Lewes, close to Brighton, lies behind Newhaven at the junction of the A26, the A27 and the A275. The town is very crowded on Bonfire Night, so park well away from the centre.

Nearest railway station: Lewes.

LICHFIELD, Staffordshire

Sheriff's Ride

Once a year on 8 September, the Feast of the Nativity of the Blessed Virgin Mary, the Sheriff of Lichfield accompanied by some forty or fifty horsemen rides round the city limits; he halts at each of the surviving boundary marks, or places where marks formerly existed, in the 16-mile circuit. This custom runs back to Tudor times, and was confirmed by a charter still in force, granted by Charles II in 1664. By this charter, the Bailiff and Brethren of Lichfield were required to choose annually, on 25 July, a Sheriff from among those citizens who were not themselves Brethren. The Sheriff in his turn was required, amongst his other duties, to tour the city boundaries annually.

At about eleven o'clock on the morning of 8 September, the Sheriff's party starts out from the Guildhall and circuits the town, a ceremony which, with various stops for refreshments and necessary formalities, takes up most of the day. On their return in the evening, they are met by the city Sword- and Mace-bearers, who conduct the Sheriff back to the Guildhall.

This traditional perambulation is a purely civic custom, and has nothing at all to do with the ecclesiastical parade of the Beating of the Bounds, to remind parishioners of the parish boundaries, which takes place in Lichfield on Ascension Day.

The town is a mile or so north of the junction of three great Midlands trunk roads – the A5, A38 and A51.

Nearest railway station: Lichfield.

LITTLE WALSINGHAM, Norfolk

Walsingham Pilgrimages

In 1061, it is said, the Lady Richeldis de Fervaques had a vision in which she was transported to the home of Christ in Nazareth, and was there told by the Virgin Mary that she must build an exact replica of the holy shrine at Little Walsingham. The Lady Richeldis accomplished her task 'with the aid of Heaven'; a holy well gushed forth healing waters and an Augustinian priory was established nearby.

Throughout the Middle Ages, Little Walsingham was one of the most important centres of pilgrimage in Britain. Thousands of pilgrims went there each year and it enjoyed the patronage of kings, among them Edward I and Henry III. For a time even the Milky Way was known as the Walsingham Way, since it seemed to point across the heavens to England's Nazareth. But at the Reformation, both shrine and priory were destroyed and of them only a few walls remain.

However, the importance of the place was never forgotten, and today there are two shrines to Our Lady of Walsingham, one Anglican, the other Roman Catholic, to which regular pilgrimages are made each weekend between Easter and October. The greatest Anglican gathering, attracting thousands of people, takes place on Whit Monday, while there is a large pilgrimage of Roman Catholic mothers on the first Tuesday in July. There is also another major Catholic pilgrimage at Assumptiontide, 15 August, and the Sunday following.

Little Walsingham, a most attractive village, is on the B1105, about 5 miles north of Fakenham, which is some 22 miles north-west of Norwich on the A1067.

Nearest railway station: Fakenham.

LIVERPOOL, Merseyside

Burning Judas

As soon as it is light on Good Friday morning, little groups of children appear on the streets in the South End of Liverpool, near the docks. Each small band carries a straw-stuffed effigy dressed in an old suit of men's clothes and with a comic mask over its face. It looks very like the traditional guy of 5 November, but is supposed to represent Judas Iscariot.

When the sun rises the leader of a group hoists the figure on a pole and knocks with it upon the upper windows of the houses while the rest of the children shout, 'Judas is short of a penny for his breakfast!' If the householders are wise, they throw out their pennies at once; certainly they will get no peace until they do so, as most realize only too well from past experience.

When they have visited as many houses as possible, the children set about the business of 'burning Judas'. Wood, straw and other fuel have been patiently collected in the preceding weeks and are now brought out. A fire is stacked and lit in the middle of the street and the effigy is thrown onto it. While it burns, the children shout, dance round the fire and throw more fuel on the flames. This rather dangerous proceeding is not liked by the police and before long, a policeman usually appears, scatters the bonfire and carries off the effigy to the police station, closely followed by its indignant owners. 'It is comic,' says one witness, 'to see a policeman with two or more

"Judases" under his arm striding off to the Bridewell and thirty or forty children of all ages crowding after him shrieking "Judas", and by this time the youngest children are thinking the policeman is Judas. . . . For a few days when a policeman is seen the cry of "Judas" is shouted after him, but it dies away after less than a week, only to be revived again next Good Friday.'

Tradition demands that the burning must take place by eleven o'clock in the morning. By noon, the fires are all out, any effigies that have escaped the police have been consumed and all that remains to be done is the counting and spending of the pennies that have been collected.

No other part of Liverpool's wide dockland area celebrates Good Friday in this way. The custom is said to have begun in the South End in the days when Spanish sailing ships came there to discharge their cargoes of fruit and wine. On Good Friday, the sailors could be seen vigorously flogging a Judas effigy round the docks and afterwards throwing it overboard.

Punishing Judas was once a widespread Good Friday practice, and is still quite well known in Spain, Portugal and some Latin-American countries. Life-size figures of wood or straw are – or were, until recently – dragged about the streets of towns and villages, beaten, kicked, cursed, spat upon and finally destroyed. On board ship, similar figures were thrashed, drowned or hanged. In April 1874, a report in *The Times* described how on Good Friday that year, a crowd of curious Londoners gathered to watch the flogging of effigies on Portuguese and South American ships in the docks. A newspaper account from 1810 records the solemn hanging of Judas on board some Spanish and Portuguese men-of-war then at Plymouth. Each ship had its own Judas figure which was left hanging until sunset (or, in one case, until Easter Sunday evening) and was then cut down, ripped to pieces and thrown into the water.

The same idea of punishment appears elsewhere in other forms. In the West of England it was once considered meritorious to break at least one piece of pottery on a Good Friday, because the jagged edges were supposed to pierce the body of Judas. The Jack-o'-Lent figure that used to be dragged about in many districts at the beginning of Lent, and that was then shot to pieces on Ash Wednesday evening or on Palm Sunday, was sometimes said to represent Judas also, though in fact this custom is more likely to have been associated, at least originally, with the age-old ritual of driving out winter.

However, the place where Judas can still be seen burning is Liverpool – and the M62 motorway takes you almost into the heart of this highly individualistic and cosmopolitan city. Where the motorway ends, follow the clear roadsigns to the city centre and the Pier Head. At the Pier Head the main dock road runs north to south along the Mersey. Turn south along the Strand for the South End dock area. The road leads past the recently created Maritime Museum, whose staff usually know where you can see the ancient ritual. Or ask the landlord of the well-restored traditional dockside pub, the Baltic Fleet, a few hundred yards south on the left. You may even find a policeman who will tell you.

LONDON

Houses of Parliament

Searching the Cellars

The memory of the Gunpowder Plot of 1605 is preserved by many cheerful customs in various parts of the United Kingdom and by one dignified ceremony that takes place in London before the Opening of Parliament.

This is the searching, by a detachment of Yeomen of the Guard, of the cellars under the Palace of Westminster, either on the evening before the Opening or, more usually, on the morning itself. Only the first and final stages of the custom are visible to the public, but there are always crowds for these scenes. The Yeomen, in their scarlet and gold uniforms, come from the Tower of London to the Princes' Chamber in the House of Lords and there, in the presence of a number of palace officials, they are given old candle-lanterns for use during their prolonged tour of the basements, vaults and cellars. Carrying their lighted lanterns and firmly ignoring the existence of the very efficient electric lighting, they search every corner and conceivable hiding place to satisfy themselves that no gunpowder barrels, bombs or infernal machines have been anywhere concealed with intent to blow up Sovereign, Lords and Commons. When they have proved by personal and careful inspection that all is well, a message is sent to the Queen, the Yeomen are given some well-earned refreshment and march back to the Tower. Parliament is then free to assemble without fear of disaster.

It need hardly be said that the safety of Parliament does not really depend upon this picturesque last-minute

ceremony. Nevertheless there was a night in 1605 when it did so depend upon a grimly earnest search through the multifarious cellars that then underran the Palace of Westminster, and it is this event which the modern ceremony is traditionally supposed to commemorate. In fact, there does not seem to be any real evidence for the connection, and some authorities think that regular inspections of the cellars did not begin until the time of the Popish Plot scare in the latter half of the seventeenth century.

However that may be, the search is only a preamble to the many other ceremonies that take place at the State Opening of Parliament in early November. Large crowds arrive – mostly via Green Park, St James's Park, or Westminster Stations – to see the arrival and departure of the Queen and other members of the Royal Family, in full regalia and in the State Coach, attended by the Household Cavalry. To ensure a good view, take your place early.

Law Courts, Strand, WC2

Horseshoes and Faggots

Two quit-rent services dating at least as

far back as the thirteenth century are annually rendered by the City of London to the Queen's Remembrancer, an official of the Royal Household. They take place at the end of October, on a day falling 'between the morrow of St Michael and the morrow of St Martin'. They are rendered in respect of two holdings, one a piece of ground called the Moors at Eardington in Shropshire and the other a tenement called the Forge in St Clement Danes parish. The exact site of the latter was uncertain for many years, a fact which did not prevent the annual discharge of the service relating to it. Now, however, the discovery of certain entries in the City's ancient documents has shown that the long-vanished Forge must have stood on, or near, the place on the Strand where Australia House now stands. In the *Great Roll of the Exchequer* for 1235, it is recorded that Walter le Brun, a farrier, was granted land in St Clement's parish on which to build a forge. For this he paid yearly six horseshoes and sixty-one nails. A further entry in the *Patent Rolls*, 1258–60, mentions the grant of additional land to Walter the Farrier, perhaps the same man, or his son, in what was then known as the Gore, a triangular patch of ground now partly covered by Australia House.

The annual quit-rent ceremony now takes place at the Law Courts or, more correctly, in the Royal Courts of Justice. It begins with the service rendered for the Moors. The 'tenants and occupiers of a piece of waste land called The Moors, in the County of Salop', are called upon to 'come forth and do your service'. The City Solicitor, representing the Corporation of London, then cuts a faggot with a hatchet, and another with a billhook, and hands these implements to the Queen's Remembrancer, who acknowledges the work done with the words 'Good Service'.

The tenants of the Forge are then summoned to do their service. The City Solicitor presents six immense horseshoes pierced for ten nails each, and counts out sixty-one nails of appropriate size. The Queen's Remembrancer says 'Good Number', and the City being now confirmed in its tenancy of these two properties for another year, the ceremony ends. Like the custom itself, the horseshoes and nails are of great age, perhaps running back to the days when Walter le Brun shod the heavy horses ridden by the Knights Templar at his forge, so conveniently situated near the Temple. They are kept during the year at the office of the Queen's Remembrancer and are temporarily restored to the City of London representative in time for the October ceremony.

Parking is always difficult in the Strand area, and it is easiest to come to the Law Courts by bus or underground. The nearest underground station is Temple.

Mansion House, EC4

The Rose Rent

An ancient quit-rent service, revived in 1924 by Rev. T. B. (Tubby) Clayton, who was then vicar of All-Hallows-by-the-Tower, Barking, is now rendered annually on Midsummer Day to the Lord Mayor of London. In the fourteenth century Sir Robert Knollys, a distinguished soldier, owned two houses standing opposite each other in Seething Lane, a narrow thoroughfare in the City of London. To join these two properties together, he built a hautpas, or gallery, between them bestriding the street. A licence to do this was granted to him and to his wife Constance by the City Corporation in 1381, in return for which he was required to render annually to the Mayor and Corporation one red rose at Midsummer.

This was clearly a straightforward rose-rent, of which many other examples can be found in different parts of Britain. A curious legend seems, however, to have grown up about this by no means unusual transaction. It is quite often said that the rose was a penalty imposed upon Sir Robert for building the hautpas without prior permission, and also, since there is nothing particularly onerous in producing one red rose in the middle of June, that the Corporation purposely made the penalty easy because of the very valuable services which Sir Robert had rendered to his country in the wars. There does not seem to be any clear evidence for this tale, nor are its details very likely.

The rose payment was duly made for a number of years and then ceased at some uncertain date, possibly when the houses concerned were demolished. Since the custom was revived in 1924, it is usual for the rose to be carried on a velvet cushion by the churchwardens of All-Hallows-by-the-Tower (or sometimes by some other chosen person) and presented to the Lord Mayor at the Mansion House.

All-Hallows-by-the-Tower is also the home of Toc H, the Christian fellowship founded in the trenches of the First World War by Rev. Tubby Clayton; the ever-burning Toc H lamp recalls the old spirit of comradeship. The nearest underground station to the church is Tower Hill, while the Mansion House is best reached by the station of the same name.

Royal Hospital, Chelsea, SW3

Founder's Day

Oak Apple Day, Royal Oak Day, Oak-and-Nettle Day, and in some places Shick Shack Day, are all traditional names for 29 May, the anniversary of Charles II's triumphal entry into London after the Restoration of 1660. Of his many adventures during his long span of misfortune and exile, it was his concealment in the oak at Boscobel which seems to have made the greatest impression upon his people. Hence the names of the festival. Oak Apple Day was for a long time an extremely popular holiday, and tended in some districts to overshadow even May Day, and to absorb some of its ceremonies. Towards the end of the last century its popularity waned somewhat and some of its customary observances were forgotten; but a number of the customs associated with the day still survive and nearly all have some connection with the oak.

Founder's Day at the Royal Hospital, Chelsea, is celebrated every year on or about 29 May. It was Charles II who

founded this 'hostel or guest house for worthy veterans of the Army who are prevented by old age or disability from earning a livelihood' in 1682. Nell Gwynn is said to have suggested the idea to him but, whether she did or not, he was ready enough to put it into practice. In the centre of the main court of Wren's splendidly austere building, there is a statue of Charles, the work of Grinling Gibbons, and this on Founder's Day is entirely covered with oak boughs. In front of it some special visitor, a member of the Royal Family or some famous soldier, stands to take the salute of the veterans marching past in their scarlet coats, all of them wearing sprigs of oak, as does the visitor. Some of the old soldiers are of course too infirm to take part in the parade, but they have their places reserved for them in the court. There they can see all that happens and take part in the final cheers for the visitors, the Founder, and the Queen.

The Royal Hospital, which Carlyle described as 'quiet and dignified and the work of a gentleman', may be visited by taking the underground to Sloane Square and walking down Royal Hospital Road to the Embankment. The veterans, commonly known as Chelsea Pensioners, in their uniforms based upon those worn during Marlborough's wars, are a familiar sight in Chelsea's streets and pubs.

St Bartholomew-the-Great, Smithfield, EC1

Butterworth Dole

On Good Friday morning, twenty-one 5p pieces are laid upon a flat stone in the churchyard for the benefit of as many poor widows, who must live in the parish. Each woman kneels in turn to pick up a coin and then steps across the stone and is given a further monetary payment and a hot-cross bun. The beneficiaries are chosen by the vicar and churchwardens. Sometimes, these days, they have difficulty finding enough people to give the dole to. Amounts, in total, can be as much as a few pounds.

The payment of this dole, known as the Butterworth Charity, is first mentioned in the churchwardens' accounts for 1686, and is often said to derive from a bequest of that year. In fact, there is nothing in the entry, or in any other parish record, to show whether the custom was then old or new, or how it came into being. The original documents relating to it have all been lost, and the date of the bequest, the donor's name and the position of his (or her) grave in the churchyard are all unknown. In the late nineteenth century it seemed probable that the charity would fail for lack of funds, but in 1887 it was saved by the generosity of a Mr Joshua Butterworth who gave a sum of money as a perpetual endowment – and his name to the dole.

It is not surprising that records should have gone missing, for the church, like St Bartholomew's Hospital nearby, was founded as long ago as 1123 by Rahere, royal jester to Henry I. There are several underground stations in the area, but the most convenient is Barbican.

St Clement Danes Church, Strand, WC2

Oranges and Lemons

Annually on 31 March, or as near as possible to that date, the Oranges and Lemons ceremony is held in the Church of St Clement Danes. The children of the nearby primary school come to the church for a short service in which the lesson is read by a child. The sermon and blessing are given by the Royal Air Force chaplain, in whose charge the church now is. When the service is ended, the tune of the traditional nursery-rhyme that begins

Oranges and lemons
Say the bells of St Clements

is played upon handbells by members of the London County Association of Change Ringers. Then as the children stream out of the building, each one is given an orange and a lemon by the chaplain and his helpers.

This charming ceremony is not old, dating only from 1920, but it is nevertheless a continuation in a new form of the centuries-old association of St Clement Danes parish church with oranges and lemons. The present church was built by Wren in the seventeenth century, but another stood upon the site as early as the tenth century and served the Danes who then lived in the neighbourhood. When lemons and oranges first came to England in the Middle Ages, they were brought upriver, and are traditionally said to have been landed close to the churchyard, which once stretched down to the shore of the Thames. They were carried thence to Clare Market, passing through Clement's Inn, where a toll had to be paid.

The children's ceremony was started in 1920 by Rev. William Pennington-Bickford, then rector of the parish. The fruit was given by London's Danish colony for distribution to the children. From then on, Oranges and Lemons Day was annually observed until the outbreak of the Second World War. The church and its famous bells were both seriously damaged in 1941 but after the war the building was restored. It became the Royal Air Force church and the crests of wartime squadrons were carved in slate and set into the pavement. The bells were rehung in 1957 and the 'Oranges and Lemons' tune is played by the bells four times every day: at 9.00 a.m., at noon, at 3.00 p.m. in the afternoon and at 6.00 p.m.

St Clement Danes – Dr Johnson's parish church – is probably best reached by way of Temple underground station.

St James's Palace, SW1

Epiphany Gifts

The gifts which the Three Kings brought to the Holy Child on the first Epiphany are commemorated every year by a royal ceremony of medieval origin. On 6 January during the Epiphany service open to the public in the Chapel Royal at St James's Palace, two Gentlemen Ushers offer gold and, even these days, frankincense and myrrh on behalf of the Queen. Silk bags, or purses, containing the gifts are laid upon an alms dish and carried to the altar rails during the offertory. The gold is now given in the form of twenty-five golden sovereigns, which are afterwards exchanged for £25 in ordinary notes; the money is distributed to the aged poor.

Until the latter part of George III's reign, the Sovereign came in person to make his offerings before the altar. During the Regency, however, when the King's mental illness made it impossible for him to perform this or any other royal duty, the presentation had to be made by proxy, and this has been the custom ever since.

St James's Palace is in Pall Mall, at the bottom of St James's Street. The nearest underground station is Green Park.

St Katherine Creechurch, Leadenhall Street, EC3

Lion Sermon

On 16 October every year a sermon known as the Lion Sermon is preached in the church in accordance with the will of Sir John Gayer, who died in 1649. He was a London merchant who was Lord Mayor of the city in 1646 and 1647 and suffered imprisonment in the latter year for his bold refusal to subsidize Parliamentary troops from City funds. The sermon commemorates his escape from deadly peril. When on one of his trading expeditions into far countries, he somehow became separated from his companions and, alone and unarmed, suddenly came face to face with a lion. In this extremity, remembering Daniel he fell on his knees and prayed for deliverance. His prayer was answered: the lion looked at him and turned away, leaving him unharmed. As a thanks-offering for that miraculous escape, he afterwards gave money for a number of charitable purposes and also provided for the annual preaching of a sermon in St Katherine Creechurch on the anniversary of his adventure. This sermon, now more than 300 years old, is still regularly preached upon that date unless it falls on a Sunday, when the sermon is transferred to the nearest weekday.

The present St Katherine Creechurch (Christchurch) dating mainly from 1628, has many associations with the life of the City. It figured in the trial of Archbishop Laud, since the High Church manner in which he conducted the church's consecration was one of the factors that led to his execution.

The nearest underground stations are Bank and Monument.

Thames Embankment

Doggett's Coat and Badge Race

The oldest sculling-race in the world is the Thames Watermen's Race for Doggett's Coat and Badge, which is rowed annually on 1 August or as near as possible to that date, from London Bridge to Chelsea. This race was founded in 1715 by Thomas Doggett, a well-known actor–manager who held strong political views and was a firm supporter of the Hanoverian dynasty. To mark the anniversary of George I's accession to the throne, he gave an orange-coloured coat and a silver badge embossed with the White Horse of Hanover (or, as he preferred to call it, 'a badge representing Liberty'), to be competed for on 1 August by six young watermen who had finished their apprenticeship during the previous twelve months. It was his wish that the race should 'be continued annually on the same day for ever'; to ensure this he left funds in the hands of the Fishmongers' Company which is still responsible for all the arrangements.

Thomas Doggett died in 1721, but his race still goes on though not always on the date he chose. Being an actor not a waterman, he made no allowance for the state of the river, and this oversight had subsequently to be rectified by fixing the event 'as near to August 1st as the tides allow'. The boats now used are racing single sculls instead of the heavier craft of his day, and the colour of the coat is now scarlet instead of orange. The Fismongers' Company has added other awards to the original bequest so that now the winner receives £10 as well as the coat and badge, and every competitor who reaches the winning post, even if belatedly, receives a prize. Eliminating heats are rowed, for the race is very popular, and there are usually many more entrants than the six permitted by the bequest. Except for these changes, and for the fact that many of the competitors may not realize that they are supposed to be honouring the memory of George I, this strenuous and testing race against the tide is just as it was when it was first rowed more than 250 years ago.

A good view of the race may be obtained anywhere along the Embankment between London Bridge and Chelsea but should you wish to see the finish, take the underground to Sloane Square or South Kensington and walk to the Albert Bridge. Details of date and times may be obtained from the Fishmongers' Company, Fishmongers' Hall, London Bridge, EC4.

Tower of London

Her Majesty's Keys

On every night of the year a ceremony, now nearly 700 years old, takes place in the Tower of London when the gates of that fortress are locked against all enemies and intruders. This is the Ceremony of the Keys or, correctly, of Her Majesty's Keys.

At 9.53 p.m. the Chief Warder, wearing his long scarlet coat and Tudor bonnet, comes from the Byward Tower carrying a candle lantern and the keys of the gates. He goes to the Bloody Tower archway, where he is met by a sergeant and four guardsmen who form the Escort to the Keys. He hands the lantern to the drummer or bugler of the Escort, and then joins the ranks. On the command of the sergeant, the whole party marches down Water Lane towards the Byward Tower archway, where they are joined by the Watchman, also scarlet-coated, who accompanies them as far as the Middle Tower and there falls out to prepare the gates for locking. The rest go on to the West Gate, where the Chief Warder, lighted by the drummer holding the lantern, locks the gate and the escort presents arms. The Middle and Byward Tower gates are locked with the same ceremony.

The company then return to the Bloody Tower archway, where they are challenged by the sentry on duty with the words 'Halt! who comes there?' The Chief Warder replies, 'The Keys,' and is asked, 'Whose Keys?' He replies, 'Queen Elizabeth's Keys.' The sentry then says, 'Advance, Queen Elizabeth's Keys, all's well.' The party passes on through the archway to a position opposite the Main Guard; the guard and escort present arms, and the Chief Warder, taking two steps forward, doffs his bonnet and says 'God preserve Queen Elizabeth!' to which all reply 'Amen.' Then, at the precise moment that the barrack clock strikes ten the bugler sounds the Last Post and the Chief Warder, taking back the lantern, carries the keys to the Queen's House, where they are left in the custody of the Resident Governor for the night.

The Ceremony of the Keys, splendid at any time, is perhaps most moving in autumn and winter when mist off the river softens the lantern's gleam and flattens the echoes from the old walls. Permission to see the ceremony may be obtained by writing about two weeks in advance to: The Resident Governor's Office, HM Tower of London, London, EC3, giving two choices of dates and enclosing a stamped addressed envelope. The nearest underground station is Tower Hill.

Tower of London

Lilies and Roses

On 21 May every year Eton College and King's College, Cambridge, honour the memory of their founder Henry VI, who died very suddenly, and was almost certainly murdered, in the Tower of London on that day in 1471. The King is generally supposed to have been killed whilst at prayer in the oratory of the Wakefield Tower, and here on the anniversary of his death the Ceremony of the Lilies and Roses now takes place. Representatives of both colleges walk in procession with Beefeaters and the Chaplain of the Tower. A short service is conducted by the latter, during which a prayer composed by Henry himself is said. A marble tablet in the oratory marks the place where the King is believed to have died; on each side of it flowers are laid, from Eton, lilies bound with pale blue silk, and from King's College white roses bound with purple ribbon. They are left there for twenty-four hours and then they are burnt.

Tower of London

Beating the Bounds

When maps were scarce, the simplest method of remembering the parish limits was to walk round them at least once a year, ensuring that everyone who took part in the perambulation had good reason to remember where the boundary marks lay. Young people especially had the route impressed upon their memories by painful physical experience. They were bumped upon stones, thrown into dividing streams or ponds, dragged through hedges and forced to climb over roofs of houses built across the lines. Afterwards they were rewarded with money, white willow wands or some other gift; for the rest of their lives they would be able to state quite definitely where any boundary mark was, should a dispute arise.

On Ascension Day in the Tower of London, the Resident Governor in full dress, the Yeomen Warders in their scarlet and gold uniform, the Chaplain of the Tower and the choirmen and boys in their red cassocks perambulate the limits of the Tower Liberty, or boundary. When one of the thirty-one Crown Boundary Marks is reached, the Chaplain calls out, 'Cursed is he who removeth his neighbour's landmark!' The Chief Warder then gives the order, 'Whack it, boys, whack it!' and the choristers enthusiastically beat the mark with their long willow wands.

The ceremony is known to have been performed as early as 1555, although at that time there was some uncertainty as to the precise limits of the Liberty. In 1687 they were clearly defined in a charter granted by James II, which now hangs in the Constable's office.

Trafalgar Square, WC2

London's Christmas Tree

The Christmas tree that now spreads its lighted and decorated branches every year in so many different countries derives from a German custom. According to one legend, it was introduced by Martin Luther who, walking at night in the woods and seeing the winter stars glittering through the branches, conceived the idea of having a candlelit tree in his house, as an image for his children of the starry heavens from whence Christ came into this world.

Christmas trees reached America before they came to England, carried there by German settlers and by Hessian soldiers in George III's army, who are said to have set them up in their camps in the American War of Independence. The first English examples of which we have a precise record are the three little trees at Panshanger, Hertfordshire, which Princess Lieven gave in 1829 for a children's party.

In 1841 Queen Victoria and Prince Albert, who is commonly thought to have introduced the custom to Britain, had a lighted tree, the first of many, at Windsor Castle. Doubtless, newspaper accounts and pictures of successive royal trees helped to make the trees better known. Even before 1841, though, Manchester people were well acquainted with the custom, for the many German merchants resident in that town had introduced it to the homes of their English neighbours.

In recent years, the Christmas tree has spread outwards from the house and into the churches and streets. Many towns have a communal tree, round which carol services are often held, in some square or park or outside the Town Hall. This custom began first in America where an illuminated tree was set up in 1909 at Pasadena in California; thence it spread across the United States and onwards to Europe and elsewhere.

In Britain, the most famous of all communal trees is the one that, since 1947, the citizens of Oslo give each Christmas to the citizens of London.

Immensely tall and brilliantly illuminated, it is set up in Trafalgar Square where it rivals Nelson's Column; it attracts thousands, both Londoners and visitors, who come to admire and to sing carols. The carol-singing is a splendid occasion but since it is so well attended, it is best to come by underground; the nearest station is Trafalgar Square.

Westminster Abbey

Royal Maundy

The distribution of the Royal Maundy takes place every year on Maundy Thursday, in years of even number normally in Westminster Abbey, and in various places throughout the country in those of odd number. Purses of money are given to as many poor women and as many poor men as there are years in the sovereign's age, the presentation being made either by the Queen herself or, if she is absent, by the Lord High Almoner acting on her behalf, or by a member of her family.

This is a very old ceremony, which once included an even older rite that is now omitted. Very early in Christian history, it was a pious custom among priests and devout persons to wash the feet of twelve poor men on this day, following the example set by Christ on the eve of His death. Exactly when this became a recognized ecclesiastical ritual is uncertain. It appears to have been known in Britain as early as AD 600, in the course of time the giving of food, money or clothes to the poor people concerned being added to the feet-washing rite. During the Middle Ages this symbolic act of humility and charity was performed by the reigning monarch and high Church dignitaries,

with the perhaps inevitable result that what had originally been a very simple ceremony gradually developed into a solemn and splendid function, full of colour and beauty.

The custom of varying the number of poor people according to the age of the sovereign seems to have begun in the Middle Ages, when the sovereign also added the robes he had worn at the celebration to his other gifts. Presumably these were sold for the recipients' benefit, since they could hardly have worn them. Mary I evidently observed this custom, for there is a record of her giving in 1556 her Maundy robe of fine purple cloth lined with marten's fur; after her time, the royal gowns were commonly redeemed by a special money payment.

James II was the last monarch known to have performed the washing rite – in 1685, when 'our gracious King James ye 2nd wash'd, wip'd, and kiss'd ye feet of 52 poor men with wonderful humility'. His successor William III had little inclination for such things, and the rite died out.

The modern celebration begins with the processional entry of clergy, officials and choristers in a blaze of scarlet, white and gold. They are followed by the Queen's Bodyguard of Yeomen of the Guard, two of whom bear the great dishes on which the leather purses are piled. After a service, the Queen, or the Archbishop of Canterbury in his capacity of Lord High Almoner, distributes the sets of purses. There are two distributions. In the first, a white purse is given to each man and a green one to each woman; these contain the allowance in lieu of clothing. In the second, the redemption money for the royal robes and the allowance for provisions are given in a red purse, and the specially minted Maundy Money is presented in a white leather purse with red thongs. The Maundy Money consists of silver penny, twopenny, threepenny and fourpenny pieces; they are legal tender; but usually they are treasured as mementoes and only rarely do they pass into circulation.

This ancient and colourful act of royal generosity is a well-attended occasion; when it is held at Westminster Abbey, it is advisable to come by bus or underground. The nearest stations are Westminster or St James's Park.

MARHAMCHURCH, Cornwall

Marhamchurch Revel

This ancient festival is held in honour of Saint Morwenna, the Celtic saint who brought Christianity to the area in the sixth century. It takes place on the Monday following 12 August, the saint's day, when a Queen of the Revel is elected from among the village schoolgirls and crowned on a spot in front of the church where Saint Morwenna's cell, or perhaps her holy well, once stood. By long-established custom, the person who performs the crowning is disguised as Father Time. After the coronation, the Queen, riding a white horse and surrounded by her attendants in fancy dress, leads round the village a procession which includes the local band. She then conducts her followers to the Revel Ground, where the children give an exhibition of country dancing; there is also Cornish wrestling, sideshows and other entertainments.

Marhamchurch, which was founded as a monastic settlement to perpetuate the teachings of Saint Morwenna, is situated on the A39 about 2 miles south-east of Bude.

Nearest railway station: Exeter.

MERIDEN, Warwickshire

Woodmen of Arden

The village of Meriden claims to be the true geographical centre of England and was once very near to the centre of the then widespread Forest of Arden. There the archery company known as the Woodmen of Arden meets to hold its Wardmotes, or medieval-style archery competitions, in June and July every year, and its Grand Wardmote in

August. As far as its records show, this company is not quite 200 years old, having been formed in 1785; but it is probable that Meriden, or its immediate surroundings, has seen the meetings of many earlier companies in the Middle Ages, when archery was of the first importance and the foresters settled their affairs at open-air gatherings in the forest's centre.

The present company is limited to eighty members. The Woodmen of Arden wear a uniform consisting of a green coat with gilt buttons, green hat, buff waistcoat and white trousers. They use a six-foot yew bow of a type known as Crecy and Agincourt, and arrows stamped according to their weight in silver, as was usual in medieval times. Their major archery competition is the Grand Wardmote, which lasts for four days at the beginning of August.

The Woodmen's headquarters are in the eighteenth-century Forest Hall by the field on the edge of the village where the competitions are held. Robin Hood is said to have taken part there. The village is 6 miles west of Coventry, just off the A45.

Nearest railway station: Coventry.

MIDGLEY, West Yorkshire

The Pace Egg Play

In the three or four days before or after Easter, or on the morning of Easter Day itself, the Pace Eggers, or Jolly Boys, still go their rounds in many districts of the English northern counties. Nowadays it is mainly children who keep up the old custom, but even eighty or ninety years ago it was young men and lads who paraded through the villages begging for eggs and other gifts, and acting the Pace Egg Play, an Easter version of the

Mumming Play. They were disguised in various ways, as befitted their ancient character as ritual performers. Often they appeared with fluttering paper streamers sewn all over their ordinary garments, or in a variety of strange costumes dictated either by personal fancy or by the parts they acted in the Pace Egg Play. Usually too their faces were blackened with soot or hidden by masks.

At Midgley, in the Calder Valley, a version of the Pace Egg Play is still acted in full by the boys of Calder High School, who wear curious stylized headdresses and beribboned costumes. They are the last of the many such teams that once performed on Good Friday in the streets of the valley towns. Elsewhere, the children who now go Pace Egging on their own rarely act the old play and are probably unaware of its existence except in a few places where its words and actions are still remembered by parents or grandparents. Quite often, however, they dress up in some fantastic manner or blacken their faces. And usually they remember one or more of the traditional begging-songs appropriate to the occasion, such as:

> Please, good mistress, an Easter egg,
> Or a flitch of bacon,
> Or a little trundle cheese
> Of your own making.

or the little verse used mostly by Cheshire children which runs:

> Please Mrs Whiteleg,
> Please to give us an Easter Egg,
> If you won't give us an Easter Egg,
> Your hens will all lay addled eggs,
> And your cocks all lay stones.

These they cheerfully chant outside the doors of the houses they visit. (See *Anglesey*, page 92.)

The village of Midgley is a few miles west of Halifax on the A646 road.

Nearest railway station: Halifax.

MINEHEAD, Somerset

The Hobby Horse

The Minehead creature is perhaps not quite so well-known as his brother of Padstow, Cornwall, but he is no less impressive. His body is formed by a frame covered by a horsecloth which has gaily coloured circles painted on it. On the flap of this frame there is a mass of short, brightly hued streamers, like a great rag mat. He has a rope tail, like that of a cow but far longer, a tall cap and a painted mask of savage aspect over his face. Once he had a horse head with snapper jaws, but that appears to have been lost.

He is known as the Sailor's Horse and lives on the quayside. He comes out on Warning Night, that is May Eve, and again on May Day itself, when he and his attendants go to Dunster Castle and all over the townships of Dunster and Minehead. In a cyclical and circular way the man who plays the horse is chosen from those who have been, or are eligible to be attendants – friends or

relatives of former attendants. It is considered an honour to perform in the ritual.

The horse was once a great deal fiercer than he is now. He used to be accompanied by two masked men, known as Gullivers, who wore tall headdresses and carried tongs and a whip, which they used to frighten people into free-giving. A man truly ungenerous, or in some way tiresome, was liable to the penalty of booting, that is of being bound with the rope tail, and struck up to ten times with a boot carried for the purpose. The Gullivers have disappeared, but booting has occurred occasionally within this century.

Formerly, household doors were left open for horse and Gullivers to enter and bring the luck of the summer to the residents, but now the horse cavorts alone in the open street and dances a few steps outside the houses that he visits.

Minehead is on Bridgwater Bay with the lovely Brendon Hills behind. It is most easily reached by the A38 from Bridgwater, or by the A358 from Taunton.

Nearest railway station: Taunton.

NORHAM, Northumberland

Blessing the Salmon
The thirty-eight salmon net fisheries on the River Tweed are annually blessed at Norham at the beginning of the fishing season on 14 February. A short open-air service is held just before midnight at the ancient fishery of Pedwell and to it, in the darkness of the February night and often in wild or snowy weather, come fishermen and others from both sides of the border. The vicar of Norham calls down a blessing upon the river itself and upon the boats, nets, fishermen, and all concerned with the thirty-eight fisheries.

The service is timed to allow the first boat of the season to be launched immediately after midnight.

In its present form, this ceremony is hardly a century old, but it is locally believed to be derived from an earlier practice. It conforms to an ancient tradition once very common amongst fishermen almost everywhere at the start of their season. In view of the known antiquity of the Pedwell fishery it is not unlikely that this comparatively modern rite is the successor of some older and now forgotten ritual once held in the same place and for the same purpose.

Norham, with its great Norman keep that figures in Scott's *Marmion*, lies on the B6470 some 3 miles to the east of the A6112, the road between Coldstream and Duns.

Nearest railway station: Berwick Upon Tweed.

NORTHAMPTON

Oak Apple Day
The townsfolk of Northampton remember Charles II on Oak Apple Day with gratitude as well as loyalty. For in 1675, when a large part of the town was destroyed by fire, he gave them a thousand tons of timber from Whittlewood Forest to build new houses, and also waived the payment of chimney tax for seven years.

Here on 29 May, the Mayor and Corporation, carrying bunches of oak apples, or acorns, and gilded leaves, lead a procession which includes schoolchildren bearing the same emblems. The procession goes from the town hall through some of the main streets to All Saints' Church, where a service is held and a charity sermon preached. At this church there is a statue of Charles II, which is decorated with oak boughs for the occasion by choristers.

This busy county town is only a mile or so east of junction 16 on the M1 motorway.

Nearest railway station: Northampton.

OAKHAM, Leicestershire

Oakham Horseshoes

When a peer of the realm comes for the first time to the manor of Oakham, in what was once the county of Rutland but which is now part of Leicestershire, tradition requires that he should pay tribute to the lord of the manor. This payment takes the form of a shoe from his horse or, failing that, a sum of money in lieu thereof.

This custom is said to date from the reign of Henry II, and to have been instituted by Wakelin de Ferrers who built Oakham Castle in about 1180. Whether he then had the right, or the power, to enforce his demands upon travelling princes as well as lesser noblemen is not clear, but certainly Elizabeth I was willing to conform to what had already become 'immemorial custom' by her time, for she contributed a shoe in 1556. She was not in fact queen at that date, but since then several reigning monarchs and their near kinsmen have done as she did, including Queen Victoria, Edward VII, George VI, the Duke of Windsor (when he was Prince of Wales), the Duke of Edinburgh and, in 1967, Queen Elizabeth II.

Originally, the shoes presented, or

substitutes bought with the compensation money, were nailed onto the outside of the castle gate where all could see them. Now they hang indoors round the walls of the Great Hall. Practically all the horseshoes displayed are in fact substitutes, some of them being very large or of fancy construction. One presented by the Prince Regent in 1814 is of immense size and made of bronze and ormolu. Many of the shoes presented more recently are gilded, ornamented and surmounted by a coronet. Each one bears the name of the giver and the date on which he or she gave it.

The old town of Oakham, with its roofed butter cross in the marketplace, lies hard by the great manmade lake of Rutland Water. Drive east along the A47 road from Leicester to Uppingham, then turn north on the A6003. Oakham is about 5 miles up the road.

Nearest railway station: Oakham.

OLNEY, Buckinghamshire

Pancake Race

One of the main events of Shrove Tuesday at Olney is the Pancake Race. A race of sorts is said to have been first run there in 1445 and to have continued intermittently ever since, with occasional lapses and revivals. The present version seems to be largely the creation of an inventive local woman and to date from no further off than the end of the Second World War.

The competitors are housewives who must be inhabitants of Olney or nearby Warrington. The rules also require them to wear aprons and to cover their heads with a hat or scarf. The course to be run is from the village square to the parish church, about 415 yards. A bell rings twice before the race, once to

poet Cowper than for its pancakes, is a large village on the A509 to the north of Newport Pagnell.

Nearest railway stations: Wolverton, Bedford.

OTTERY ST MARY, Devon

Tar-barrel Rolling

On Guy Fawkes night, 5 November, the roads of Ottery St Mary are barred to traffic and nine burning tar barrels are carried through the town at intervals during the evening, each one starting from a different point. The first is lit outside the factory at 8.15 p.m. As soon as it is well alight a man with his hands and arms swathed in stout sacking picks it up and, holding it above his head, runs with it as far as he can down the street. When the heat becomes unbearable, he sets it down and lets it roll along the ground. Another man then picks it up and carries it onwards until he too can do no more. This goes on until the barrel becomes impossible to hold, after which it is rolled until it finally disappears in a sheet of flame. The same process is repeated with the other barrels in turn. The last of the nine is timed to reach the end of the course at about 11.45 p.m., when the lively celebrations, which include the burning of a guy upon a huge bonfire, come to an end. There is also a 'junior' barrel-rolling at 4.00 p.m., when four or five smaller barrels are lighted and carried by boys whose hands and arms are protected in the same way as those of the young men, with sacking.

warn the women to make their pancakes and again to bid them assemble in the square, each one carrying a frying pan with the cooked cake in it. Finally the Pancake Bell is rung once more to start them running.

The pancakes have to be tossed three times during the race and some inevitably land in the road, but such mishaps do not disqualify the runner who is allowed to pick up a dropped pancake and toss it again. At the church door, the vicar waits to greet the breathless women and to award the winner and the runner-up a prayerbook as a prize. With him stands the verger who has the right to claim a kiss from the winner and is usually given her pancake as well. Then all the pans are laid round the font in the church and a short service of blessing is held. Pancakes have long been a feature of Shrove Tuesday, a traditional means of using up stocks of butter, eggs and flour before the Lenten fast begins.

Since 1950, a similar race has been run on the same day at Liberal, Kansas, and there is keen competition in running times between these two widely separated townships. Olney, more famed for its lacemakers and for the

Ottery St Mary is situated in beautiful farming country some 5 miles inland from Sidmouth and a little to the south of the A30 Honiton–Exeter road.

Nearest railway station: Honiton.

OXFORD

May Singing

Every year at six o'clock on May morning, the choristers of Magdalen College, Oxford, go to the top of the Magdalen Tower and greet the sunrise with a Latin hymn. In spite of the early hour, there is always a large crowd gathered on the bridge below to hear the singing and the pealing of the tower bells which follows. Immediately afterwards, morris dancers from Oxford and Headington run through the streets and dance at various fixed points in the city.

The origin of the custom is mysterious. It is often said that a requiem Mass for Henry VII used to be sung on the tower on 1 May and that when this practice ceased at the Reformation, the present custom was substituted for it. There is not, however, any real evidence for this story. The seventeenth-century Oxford historian, Anthony Wood, said that in his day, the choristers 'do, according to an ancient custom, salute Flora every year on the first of May at four in the morning, with vocal music of several parts'. He added that this, being sometimes well performed, 'hath given great content to the neighbourhood, and auditors underneath'.

It still does, but what the 'auditors underneath' hear today is not a concert as in Wood's time. The change came more or less accidentally in the late eighteenth century. On one very wet May Day, the choristers were an hour late in reaching the tower top and hastily substituted 'Te Deum Patrem colimus', a hymn which they all knew very well, for whatever they ought to have been singing. This hymn, dating from the seventeenth century, written by Dr Thomas Smith and set to music by Benjamin Rogers, was part of the college grace. It has been sung on May Day morning ever since that first emergency rendition. It has been suggested that the custom of May Singing on the tower may have started as an inaugural ceremony, in the form of a secular concert, connected with the completion of the tower in 1509.

Magdalen (pronounced 'Maudlin' since the Middle Ages) College is at the north end of the High Street, known as the High, just before Magdalen Bridge.

Needle and Thread Ceremony

A rebus – a kind of visual pun – on the name of Robert de Eglesfield, founder of the Queen's College, Oxford, forms the basis of a little ceremony which takes place every year on New Year's Day in that college.

Eglesfield founded the college in 1341. He provided for a provost and twelve fellows, in honour of Christ and the twelve Apostles. They were to wear crimson mantles, typifying the Blood of Christ, and they were to dine in Hall seated on one side only of the high table, with the provost in the midst, in imitation of traditional pictures of the Last Supper. He also directed that on New Year's Day every member of the college should receive from the bursar a needle filled with coloured thread. This made a rebus – 'Aiguille et fil' – on his name, Eglesfield, and as such was to be a little memorial of a man for whom the existence of the company that shares in the ceremony and the building in which it takes place might seem memorial enough. As New Year's Day falls in vacation, not all the members of the college are in Oxford then, but to those who are, and to the fellows and their guests, the bursar hands the threaded needle, saying to each one as he does so, 'Take this and be thrifty.'

The Needle and Thread Ceremony is not open to the public, but strollers in the High on New Year's Day may catch a glimpse of the sumptuously attired provost and fellows.

St Giles' Fair

The patronal festival of any parish church is primarily a religious affair, but in many villages it is and has been for centuries a local secular holiday as well, celebrated with sports and games and sometimes an unofficial fair to which showmen came. In northern and Midland England this holiday is usually known as the wake, from the obsolete custom of 'waking', or watching, in the church during the night before a holy day.

In a number of instances up and down the country, the secular aspects of the celebrations have survived long after their original purpose has faded from general memory; so tenacious are these unofficial fairs that they have sometimes outlived the true charter fairs of the district. St Giles' Fair in Oxford is an example of this. It is held annually on the Monday and Tuesday after the first Sunday after St Giles' Day (1 September) in the two or three streets nearest to the ancient church of that saint. Thousands of people come every year without realizing that they are actually attending the old Wakes of Walton.

When the parish comprising the manor of Walton lay outside the boundaries of Oxford, it had its wake like other parishes, and no doubt this was originally quite a humble affair. By 1573, however, it had grown into a fair of considerable size, attracting stall-holders and traders from a wide area. Today, St Giles' Fair is still one of the chief pleasure fairs of the south Midlands and has cheerfully outlived the five charter fairs once held in the city, all of which, sadly, have now vanished.

PADSTOW, Cornwall

Obby Oss

On May Day, the famous Hobby Horse comes out to meet the summer. This is a horse of the 'horse and rider' type, locally known as Obby Oss or Old Oss, a spectacular beast who attracts hundreds of people to the town every year. He wears a hoop-shaped frame, about 6 feet in diameter and covered with black tarpaulin, which completely hides his human form. In front of the hoop is a small wooden horse's head, with snapper jaws, but the horseman's own head is hidden by a ferocious mask surmounted by a tall cap. Old Oss has several attendants who follow him about the streets, but the most important is the Teaser or Club-man who carries a padded club and wears grotesque clothes which vary in pattern from year to year.

The May festival at Padstow begins on the night before May Day, when the Mayers go round the town singing the 'Night Song' outside the principal houses. They stand outside the house, serenading the tenant and his wife by name, and his family, and singing:

Rise up, Mrs ——, all in your gown of green,
For Summer is I-comen in today.
You are as fair a lady as waits upon the Queen,
In the merry month of May!

There are many verses of the song, and not all of them are personal greetings.

In the morning, the Old Oss comes out of the Golden Lion Inn, which is his headquarters and the place where his accoutrements are kept during the rest of the year, accompanied by the Teaser. He sets off capering and gambolling through the streets; he chases the girls and sometimes corners one of them against a wall and covers her with his huge tarpaulin skirt. This is supposed to bring her a husband if she has not got one already, or a baby within the year if she has. Once, the inside of the cloth was smeared with blacklead, which left a mark upon the girl's face or dress as a sign of the good fortune to come, but this has not been done for many years now.

Every now and then during the proceedings the Oss dies a magical death. The lively music of the 'Night Song' changes to the slower and sadder 'Day Song', and the Mayers and most of the onlookers sing:

O, where is St George? O, where is he O?
He's out in his long-boat, all on the salt sea O.
Up flies the kite, down falls the lark, O,
Aunt Ursula Birdwood, she had an old ewe,
But it died in her own Park, O.

The Oss sinks to the ground as though he were dying and lies there while the Teaser gently strokes his head with his club. He has gone and the strange song, though its words have become quite incomprehensible by now, is plainly his dirge. Then suddenly the music changes once more, the Oss leaps up high in the air and off he goes again, as full of life as ever.

For the past fifty years or so there has been a second Hobby Horse, almost a replica of the traditional one, who has his own Teaser and followers. This is the Temperance, or Blue Ribbon, or Peace Horse, who came into being at about the end of the First World War. Although they were once rivals, the two horses now live amicably together and do not encroach upon each other as they run through the town. They meet only in the late afternoon in the market square, where after an interval of some years, the maypole once more proudly stands, too tall for ribbon streamers but gaily decorated with garlands and flags and bunches of fresh spring flowers.

Padstow is on the A389 on the south shore of the Camel estuary, and is best reached by way of Launceston and Bodmin. The Horses are a very popular attraction and those needing parking space should come early.

Nearest railway station: Bodmin Road.

PAINSWICK, Gloucestershire

Clipping the Church

This is a dance-like ceremony in which the people of the parish 'clasp' or embrace their church by joining hands and moving round it in a wide ring. It is really a spring ritual, usually associated with Easter or Shrove Tuesday, but in some parishes it is, or was, performed on the patronal festival or on some other appropriate date.

At Painswick the church is clipped on the Sunday nearest 19 September, the Feast of the Nativity of Our Lady (Old Style). The children of the parish walk in procession to St Mary's Church and there, holding hands, they encircle the building, advancing towards it and retreating three times, while the 'Clipping Hymn' is sung. Afterwards a special sermon is preached from a small doorway in the tower to a large crowd gathered outside to listen. Formerly when the service was over, the children used to rush down the road towards the Old Vicarage, shouting 'Highgates!', a word of which no one knows the meaning and for which a variety of interpretations have been suggested, but that part of the celebration is now obsolete.

In 1897 the vicar published a pamphlet suggesting that the clipping ceremony was a direct descendant of the ancient *Lupercalia* festival which the pagan Romans observed on 15 February and which included the sacrifice of goats and a young dog, as well as a wild rushing through the streets of scantily clad youths armed with goatskin thongs. He believed that the children's flight down the road might have sprung from some vague folk memory of this part of the pagan ritual, and that the mysterious word 'Highgates' was probably a corruption of the Greek *aig-aitis*, derived from *aig*, a goat, and *aitis*, an object of love.

He also considered the curious custom of making 'puppydog pies' at Clipping-time had its roots in the dog sacrifice of the *Lupercalia*. These pies are round cakes crowned with almond paste that contain a small china figure of a dog, but tradition has it that originally they were filled with the cooked flesh of puppies.

Another curious local tradition concerns the ninety-nine clipped yew trees in the churchyard of St Mary's: it is said that whenever a hundredth tree is planted among the original ninety-nine, it fails to grow. The village is about 3 miles north-east of Stroud on the A46 road.

Nearest railway station: Stroud.

PRESTON, Lancashire

Preston Guild

Once in every twenty years, in the week following the Feast of St John the Baptist on 29 August, the borough of Preston in Lancashire holds the splendid civic festival which is known as Preston Guild. This celebration is certainly 600 years old, and may be older, since it began as a customary meeting of the medieval Guild Merchant, which appears to have existed by prescriptive right before the town received its first charter. There is a Preston Guild due in 1992.

The most important ceremonies are still the meeting of the Guild Court and the procession of the burgesses, Masters and Wardens of Companies, and of the Guild Mayor to the parish church, where a special sermon is preached. There are also colourful processions through streets decorated with flags and banners and, during the week-long festivities, balls, receptions, concerts, a lively pleasure fair and many other entertainments and gaieties.

At the meeting of the Guild Court, the charters granted to the borough by various monarchs are recited, a roll call is taken of the existing Free Burgesses, who answer their names in person or by proxy, and new freemen are admitted. Originally, this meeting was necessary for the transaction of the legal business of the Guild Merchant and the renewal of the burgesses' trading privileges. In the Middle Ages, those privileges were very important and jealously guarded. The guilds were extremely powerful fraternities, exercising authority over every aspect of the town's commerce and providing strong protection and a virtual trading monopoly for their members. Here, as in many other medieval guild towns, no outsider could buy or sell goods without permission, except during the annual fairs when the normal guild regulations were suspended so long as 'the Glove was up'. A glove or wooden hand exposed in some prominent position where everyone could see it was a sign that a fair was in progress and that outside merchants could safely enter the town and trade there for as long as the fair lasted.

A by-law passed in 1616 ruled that if any Preston householder admitted an outsider whom the authorities considered 'no fytt person to inhabite' their town, that outsider had to leave within a month of notice being served upon him – and his host had to see that he did so – or else pay a fine of 6s. 8d. a week for so long as he remained.

Before 1562 Preston Guild seems to have been held at irregular intervals. The earliest celebration of which there is a clear record was in 1329 and there were others in 1397, 1415, 1459, 1501, 1543 and 1562. It was then decided that the festival should take place every twenty years and this has been the custom ever since. There was a moment of danger in 1842. The exclusive privileges of the Free Burgesses had already dwindled considerably, and the Municipal Reform Act of 1835 had swept away the last remaining traces of the Guild Merchant's old importance. When Preston Guild fell due in 1842, there was much debate as to whether it was worthwhile to hold it that year – or ever again. Fortunately, the town authorities decided that it was, though as a concession to the abolitionists, its length was shortened from a fortnight to a week. Exactly a century later, the 1942 celebrations had to be postponed

because of the Second World War; but the belated Guild festival was duly held in 1952 and again in 1972, and there is no reason to suppose that the regrettably distant and other festivals will not follow in their normal twenty-year sequence.

One of the many Easter egg ceremonies still celebrated in Britain takes place in Preston: the annual Easter Monday egg-rolling in Avenham Park. Very large crowds of adults and children congregate and thousands of gaily coloured hard-boiled eggs can be seen rolling and bouncing down the steep grassy hillside towards the River Ribble. Here it is usual to bring oranges to eat with the broken eggs, and sometimes these are rolled as well. This is a purely modern innovation, intended simply to increase the fun; but perhaps the addition of these golden, sun-like globes is not altogether inappropriate in a custom which is sometimes said to have been a solar rite.

Egg-rolling flourishes in many parts of northern England, Scotland, Ulster and the Isle of Man. In some districts it is a competitive game, the winner being the player whose egg rolls furthest without being damaged; more usually the fun consists simply of rolling and then eating the eggs.

There is easy motorway access to Preston, which is just west of junction 31 of the M6, north of where it merges with the M61 from Manchester.

Nearest railway station: Preston.

READING, Berkshire

Maidservants' Charity

This charity, whose recipient is rather curiously chosen by the casting of lots, is still distributed annually in this Thames-side town. By his will, dated 30 June 1611, John Blagrave the mathematician provided for the payment of twenty nobles to 'one poor maiden servant who should have served dwelt, or continued in any one service within any of the three parishes of Reading, in good name and fame five years at the least, for her preferment in marriage'. To be sure of fairness in awarding the money, three duly qualified girls were to be chosen to compete by the casting of lots, 'yearly, for ever, upon Good Friday'. This is still done, though not now on Good Friday, nor in the town hall, the original place where the lots were cast. The award is still £20 but the stigma of domestic service has gone. Nowadays the reward is for good work, pure and simple. The girls now go to St Mary's Church House on the Thursday after Easter and cast their lots there for the prize.

Nearest railway station: Reading.

RIPON, North Yorkshire

The Hornblower

At Ripon the Mayor's Hornblower sounds the city horn each and every night at nine o'clock, four times in the marketplace and once outside the Mayor's house. This custom is believed locally to run back to Anglo-Saxon times. Before Ripon had a mayor, it had a Wakeman, whose ancient office is commemorated in the city motto painted in large letters across the front of the Town Hall: 'Unless Ye Lord Keep Ye Cittie, Ye Wakeman Waketh in Vain.' He was responsible for the preservation of good order and the protection of the citizens against robbery and violence, from nine o'clock at night to sunrise. If anyone during that time suffered loss or damage which could be proved to be due to lack of care on the part of the Wakeman and his assistants, compensation could be claimed.

One of the Wakeman's duties, according to a document of 1400, was to sound the horn every night at the four corners of the Market Cross as a form of curfew, and also as a signal that his night watch had begun. He also had to blow it on the five Horn Days. These were originally Candlemas Day, Easter, one of the Rogation days, the Feast of St Wilfrid on 12 October and the Feast of St Stephen on 26 December. They are celebrated now on Easter Sunday, Whit Sunday, August Bank Holiday, Christmas Day and Mayor's Sunday.

When Hugh Ripley, the last Wakeman, became the first Mayor of Ripon in 1604, an official Hornblower was appointed; by him and his successors the horn ritual was, and still is, performed. In 1955 the office was duplicated so as to allow the holders to leave the city for an occasional holiday. Previously this had been impossible, since the horn had to be blown every night of the year and only the official Hornblower was permitted (and perhaps only he was competent) to blow it.

Ripon has had three horns during its long history. The one used now is not old, dating only from 1864 when it replaced another which had been in continuous use since 1690. The oldest of the three, which is said to have been first blown in AD 886, is preserved among the city's treasures, being brought out only on ceremonial occasions and on the five Horn Days. At such times it is not sounded but is carried in procession by the Sergeant-at-Mace, attached to a magnificent baldric adorned with heavy silver medallions showing the coats-of-arms and badges of former Wakemen and Mayors. The office of Wakeman was supplanted by that of Mayor in 1604. The Hornblower is a municipal servant and is paid. He is appointed by the council, presumably for his ability to blow the horn.

The thirteenth-century Wakeman's House, official residence of the holder of that office, stands in a corner of the city's marketplace and contains a small museum. The horn is sounded at the foot of a 90-foot obelisk in the square, which is a focal point for Ripon's narrow, winding streets.

The town is about 25 miles to the north-west of York on the A61 road, which is accessible from the great A1 trunk road.

Nearest railway stations: Harrogate, Leeds and York.

RIVER THAMES, Southwark Bridge to Henley

Swan Upping

This ancient custom takes place annually in the week beginning on the third Monday in July, when the young swans of the river between London and Henley are rounded up, caught and marked with the swan-marks of their different owners. This process, which takes several days, is carried through by the Royal Swanherd and the Swan Wardens of the Dyers' and the Vintners' Companies of the City of London, with their attendants, and is now all that actively remains of the once-elaborate ritual connected with the ownership of every swan in England.

The mute swan was, and is, a royal bird, and seems to have been so since at least as early as the twelfth century, and

possibly earlier. All swans therefore belonged to the Crown, and no subject might own any unless the privilege of doing so had been specially bestowed upon him by the sovereign. From time to time such grants were made by the reigning king to favoured individuals or corporate bodies, and with them a distinctive swan-mark whereby ownership of the birds could be clearly recognized.

Although various secular landowners and monastic houses once enjoyed swan rights on the River Thames, there are now only two non-royal swan-owners on that river. These are the two great City Livery companies, the Dyers, to whom rights were granted in 1473, and the Vintners, who received theirs at some time between 1472 and 1483. On the first day of the Upping, the Swan Wardens maintained by the two companies, with their uniformed assistants, meet the Royal Swanherd with his helpers at Southwark Bridge, whence all travel together up the river as far as Henley, in six rowing boats. The Royal Swanherd's boat leads the way flying two flags, one of which has the Queen's initials and a crown upon it and the other a swan with raised wings. The other royal boat and the two provided by each of the companies fly only one flag apiece, those of the companies displaying their arms as well as swans.

As the boats make their slow way upriver, the Uppers catch and examine some 600 birds, a task that calls for considerable skill and does not lack excitement, since swans are not known to be docile creatures. The existing markings of the adult birds are examined to determine ownership and the cygnets of each family are similarly marked, with nicks cut in their beaks – one nick for the Dyers' birds and two for those of the Vintners. The well-known inn sign the Swan with Two Necks is said to be a corrupt version of the Vintners' mark. If the cygnets are of mixed parentage, the cob belonging to one owner and the pen to another, half the brood receive their father's markings and the other half those of their mother. If the numbers are uneven, the odd cygnet is marked like the cob.

The Queen's swans are rounded up and examined like the rest but they are not marked. It is unnecessary that they should be since all unmarked swans on the Thames are hers by prerogative, including any which may happen to stray there on their own from other waters.

This marvellous custom can be observed between Southwark and Henley every year.

ST BRIAVELS, Gloucestershire

Bread and Cheese Scramble

At St Briavels small pieces of bread and cheese are distributed every year to the inhabitants of the village on Whit Sunday, immediately after the evening service in the parish church is ended. The food is carried in baskets to a narrow lane near the church, along which runs a high stone wall. From the top of this wall, the pieces are flung to the people waiting in the roadway below and as they fall, they are scrambled for with a great deal of lively pushing and laughter. At one time the distribution took place in the church itself. A writer in 1816 recorded that 'after the service, bread and cheese is flung from the galleries inside the church among the congregation, the parson coming in for his share as he left the pulpit'. After 1857 the scramble was transferred to the churchyard, the baskets having been emptied from the top of the tower; as this practice resulted in some damage to the graves, the ceremony was eventually moved once more, this time to its present site in the nearby lane.

The due observance of the custom is said to be necessary to maintain the commoners' rights of grazing, and of cutting timber in Hudnall's Wood. The privileges appear to be of considerable age. The liberty to take wood from 'the Wood of Hodenhales' was evidently enjoyed by the men of St Briavels in the late thirteenth century, for it is mentioned in the record of a perambulation of the Forest of Dean in 1281–2; probably it was already in existence in King John's reign when Humphrey de Bohun, son of the Earl of Hereford, ceded all his rights in the forest to that monarch. The commoners' rights, however, appear to have been specially safeguarded in the transfer. They survived all the changes of later centuries, including an attempt by Cromwell to usurp them during the Commonwealth; after the Restoration of Charles II, they were confirmed by Act of Parliament.

Exactly how, or when, they were first acquired is not now known. There is a local tradition that they were won for the people by some undated Countess of Hereford who rode naked through the parish, as Lady Godiva did for a similar good cause through the streets of Coventry. This unlikely legend, for which there is no evidence whatsoever, is still occasionally repeated but it is unlikely that anyone has any real faith in it today.

The village is perched high on a bluff above the Wye Valley and youth hostellers can stay in the magnificent gate-house of its ruined thirteenth-century castle. Follow the B4228 road north from Chepstow for 5 miles or so.

Nearest railway station: Chepstow.

ST COLUMB MAJOR, Cornwall

Shrovetide Hurling
The ancient Cornish hurling game is played every Shrove Tuesday at St Columb Major, near Newquay. A ball made of applewood and coated in sterling silver is passed from hand to hand before the game starts, bringing luck, it is said, to all who touch it. The goals are 2 miles apart at different ends of the town, and any number of people can participate. They divide themselves into two teams, the Townsmen and the Countrymen. The ball is thrown up, then hurled or carried (never kicked) through the streets of the town. One goal finishes the game, and the person who has scored it is carried back shoulder-high to celebrate in the town. The contest is similar to the Shrovetide game played in St Ives (see below).

Nearest railway station: Newquay.

ST IVES, Cambridgeshire

Dicing for Bibles
Here, six bibles are annually diced for by twelve children, according to the will of Dr Robert Wilde. In 1675 he left £50, the income from which was to be spent upon bibles, which were then to be diced for at Whitsun by poor children 'of good report . . . and able to read the Bible'. A piece of land, still called Bible Orchard, was bought and the rent used to buy the books. The contest takes place in the presence of the vicar, six of the competitors belonging to the Church of England, the other six being Nonconformists. Originally the dice were thrown upon the altar of the parish church, but this ceased in about 1880 and a table near the chancel steps was used instead. After 1918 the custom was transferred to the local church school until 1963, when the Rev. R. O. Jennings restored it to its earlier form, so that the table by the chancel steps was (and is) once again used.

This St Ives – which, not the Cornish village, is the place associated in traditional rhyme with the man who had seven wives – is 7 miles east of Huntingdon on the A1123.

Nearest railway station: Huntingdon.

ST IVES, Cornwall

Feasten Monday Hurling
Shrovetide football, traditional in many parts of the country, has been replaced by hurling at St Ives. Hurling is an ancient Cornish game, once very popular, in which the ball used is about the size of a cricket ball, made of cork or light wood and thinly covered with silver. It is thrown up at the beginning of a match and then tossed, hurled or carried over the ground – but never kicked.

The game takes place on Quinquagesima Monday, which is also Feasten Monday and is the day before Shrove Tuesday. Tradition says that on Quinquagesima Sunday, the patronal festival, St Ia landed in Cornwall after her flight from Ireland on a leaf.

This game was originally played all through the town, but was transferred later to the beach. The mayor stood on the West Pier and threw the silver ball to the waiting crowd below. In 1939 it was moved to the public park, where it is still played.

A similar game is played through the streets of St Columb Major, about 30 miles away near Newquay, on Shrove Tuesday.

Nearest railway station: St Ives.

The Knillian

This Knillian is a celebration held every five years here on 25 July, the Feast of Saint James the Great. It was founded by John Knill, once Collector of Customs in the district, who in 1797, drew up a complicated deed of trust whereby certain monies were settled upon the mayor and burgesses of the borough for the provision of doles to various types of poor people at five-yearly intervals. The deed also provided for the perpetual upkeep of the Mausoleum, now known as Knill's Steeple, which he had built in 1782 on the top of Worvas Hill. This is a triangular granite pyramid 50 feet high, which serves as a landmark for seamen. Knill intended it to be his tomb but when he died in 1811, he was in London and he was buried in St Andrew's Church, Holborn.

The trust provided for various different doles; £5 was to be divided among ten little girls, none of them to be more than ten years old and all children of seamen or tinners, who were to go on the appointed day to the Mausoleum and dance there for not less than fifteen minutes, and then sing the 'Old Hundredth' to the tune used in the parish church in Knill's time. They were required to wear white cockades, and so was the fiddler who played for them and who received £1 for his service; £2 was to be paid to two widows aged sixty-four or upwards, who accompanied the children and had to 'certify to the trustees that the ceremonies have been duly performed'; £3 went to the married couple, widow or widower, sixty years old or more, who had raised the largest family of legitimate children without receiving help from the parish; the same sum was given to the best knitter of fishing nets, and to the best curer and packer of pilchards (for centuries a mainstay of the local economy) for export, and £2 10s. each to the two follower-boys judged to have behaved most excellently in the previous fishing season; £10 was to serve as a wedding portion for a girl whose marriage had taken place within a stated period; other gifts, including gifts to local friendly societies, and £10 to provide a dinner for the trustees, were also made.

The Knillian was first celebrated in 1801 and it has been kept up ever since. Certain alterations have had to be made in the payments, for the decline of the pilchard fishery has done away with the follower-boys and the award for the best packer of pilchards has had to be replaced by one for the best packer of any kind of fish.

Knillian Day is a serious festival in St Ives. Hundreds of people come to see the children dance and watch the presentation of the money to the various beneficiaries. Between ten and eleven o'clock in the morning, a long procession winds its way up the steep hill to the Mausoleum. In it walk the mayor and town officials in their robes of office, the trustees, two sergeants-at-mace, the father of the largest family and others who are to receive gifts, the white-cockaded fiddler and the ten little girls in their white dresses and rosettes. The monument is danced round, the 'Old Hundredth' and 'Shall Trelawney Die?' are sung, and the mayor calls upon the two widows to bear witness that everything has been done according to the founder's wish. When they have done so, the little girls are given 50p each, and the rest of the money is distributed. Then the procession re-forms and, led by the fiddler, goes down the hill into the town, not to be seen again for another five years. It is all tremendous fun; and if the money is no longer as important as it used to be, everyone has had a splendid day.

Motorists driving down the A30 on 25 July 1986 may find a diversion to St Ives a rewarding experience, for that is the next occasion on which the Knillian is due to be held.

Nearest railway station: St Ives.

ST JOHN'S, Isle of Man

Tynwald Day

One of the most important days in the Manx calendar is Tynwald Day, which falls on 5 July, Old Midsummer Day. On that date every law which has been passed by the Manx Parliament during the preceding year has to be promulgated from the Tynwald Hill in Manx and English. Formerly, each one was read in full in both languages, but since 1865 only the titles and abstracts are given. Until this reading has been done, no new law has any legal force in the island.

Tynwald Hill is an artificial mound built upon an open space at St John's, a village about 3 miles to the south-east of Peel. The mound is 12 feet high, circular in form and has four terraces around it at 3-foot intervals. The word 'Tynwald' is devised from the Norse *thing-vellir*, which means a place where a thing, or public assembly, was held. The Scandinavian Thing was a democratic gathering, usually held in an open space away from houses or villages, to which people came from all over the region affected by it and lived in temporary booths. Here new laws were enacted, disputes settled, and judgement pronounced upon criminals. The Isle of Man was subject to Viking rule once, and one of the relics of that time is the Tynwald Ceremony still held at Midsummer.

Exactly how old it is in its present form is not certain, but the earliest known description of it, in a document dating from 1417, differs only a little from the present proceedings. The document is quoted in *Statutes and Ordinances of the Isle of Man* (1792):

This is the Constitution of the old Time how the Lord should be governed on the Tynwald Day: First he is to come thither in his royal Array, as a King ought to do, by the Prerogatives and Royalties of the Land of Man, and upon the Tynwald Hill sit in a chair covered with a royal Cloth and Cushions, and his Visage to the East, and his Sword before him, holden with the Point upwards, his Barons in the third Degree sitting beside him, and his beneficed Men and Deemsters before him, and his Clerk, Knights, Esquires and Yeomen about him, and the worthies of the Land to be called in before the Deemsters, if the Lord will ask any Thing of them, and to hear the Government of the Land and the Lord's Will, and the Commons to stand without the Circle of the Hill with three Clerks in their surplices. . . . Then the chief Coroner, that is the Coroner of Glenfaba, shall make a Fence upon Pain of Life and Limb, that no Man shall make any Disturbance, or stir, in the Time of Tynwald, or any Murmer, or rising in the King's Presence, upon Pain of hanging and drawing; and all the Barons, worthiest Men and Commons, to make Faith and Fealty to the Lord: and then to proceed in whatsoever Matters are there to do in Felony and Treason, or other Matters that touch the Governance of the Island.

Today the ceremonies are very much the same as they were when that document was written. The Lieutenant Governor, representing the Queen, attends a service at St John's Church and then goes in procession to the Tynwald Hill. The thirteenth-century sword of state is carried before him, point upwards. He mounts to the highest of the four platforms on the hill and sits in a red velvet chair facing eastwards. The Bishop of Soder and Man, the last of the Island Barons, sits beside him, and around them stand the two Deemsters and the other members of the Council. The members of the House of Keys – the elected house of the Manx Parliament – assemble on the platform below; on the third platform are the clergy, the High Bailiffs, and members of the bar, and on the fourth, minor officials of various kinds. The ordinary people of the island stand on the grass all round the hill.

The court is 'fenced', as of old, by the Coroner of Glenfaba, who calls upon all present to refrain from brawls, quarrels and every kind of disturbance for so long as it is sitting. When this has been done, the Coroners are sworn in and the main business of the day – the reading of the titles and abstracts in Manx and English of all laws passed during the year – takes place. The people signify their consent to what has been done in their name by giving three cheers for the Queen. The procession then re-forms and the court returns to St John's Church, where the bills are signed by the Lieutenant Governor and the ceremonies come to an end.

In recent times – during which the island celebrated 1000 years of Tynwald rule – these formal proceedings have become the focal point of a day-long festival, with a fair and displays of Manx dancing and music. The friendly and hospitable island is a most popular holiday resort and regular car ferries sail from Liverpool and Heysham on the mainland to the capital, Douglas. St John's is on the opposite side of the island, but still barely a 10-mile drive away.

SCARBOROUGH, North Yorkshire

Skipping at Shrovetide

On Shrove Tuesday afternoon, the people of Scarborough – men, women and children – go down to the foreshore to skip. At noon on this day, the Pancake Bell (which now hangs in the museum) is rung and between one o'clock and half-past two, the people begin to drift down to the beach; they stay there skipping until teatime. This is an entirely spontaneous gathering; the police, it is true, do recognize it by closing the foreshore road to all but the most essential traffic but otherwise there is nothing whatever organized about it.

Skipping, besides being an ancient magical game associated with the sowing and upbringing of the seed in springtime, is known to have been played on barrows on Palm Sunday and Good Friday during the Middle Ages.

Scarborough, a delightful seaside town, is reached by the A64 road from York.

Nearest railway station: Scarborough.

SEDGEFIELD, County Durham

Street Football

A game of traditional free-for-all football is played in Sedgefield on Shrove Tuesday. Two teams of villagers take part – anyone can join in – and the 'pitch' is 500 yards long, the goals being a pond at one end and a stream at the other. The ball is provided by the verger, who kicks it off at 1.00 p.m., and the game continues until one side or the other scores a goal.

The village is 5 miles or so to the north-west of Stockton-on-Tees; turn east off the A1(M) road at its junction with the A689.

Nearest railway stations: Bishop Auckland, Stockton-on-Tees.

SHEBBEAR, Devon

Turning the Devil's Boulder

A curious ceremony of uncertain age and origin is annually performed in this north Devon village on the night of 5 November. Just outside the east gateway of the churchyard stands an ancient oak tree, said to be a thousand years old, and under it lies a large stone known as the Devil's Boulder. This stone is turned every year by the bellringers, who first go to the belfry and ring a loud, jangled peal on the bells and then go out to the stone where,

armed with crowbars, they perform their ritual task. Local tradition says that if this is not done, serious misfortune will overtake the parish during the following year.

When this ceremony was first performed, or why, is not known. It has nothing to do with the Gunpowder Plot in spite of the fact that it takes place on Guy Fawkes' Night, and it is almost certainly older than that comparatively recent conspiracy. The boulder itself is apparently an erratic, one of those alien rocks of a geological type foreign to the locality that were left behind by the retreating ice at the end of the Ice Age. Such intruders are found in numerous places and usually they are associated in legend with Satan, or with giants. This one is supposed to have been dropped onto its present site by the Devil, whose power to harm the village can only be averted by the annual turning and by the discordant peal rung beforehand. One of the few good things that tradition tells us about demons and their kin is that they do not, apparently, like loud noises.

Another local legend says that the Devil's Boulder was quarried at Henscott, a village about a mile and a half from Shebbear across the River Torridge, for use as the foundation stone of a new church. During the night it vanished, and was found next day at Shebbear. Its owners retrieved it but on the following night the same thing happened; so it went on for a long time. Finally the Henscott people grew tired of rolling an irregularly shaped boulder of considerable weight over a mile and a half of rough ground every day and decided to give up the unequal struggle against an obviously supernatural opponent. When, therefore, the stone was once again miraculously transported to Shebbear on the night of 5 November, it was left lying where it was found and, except for the ritual turning on the anniversary of that day, it has not since then been moved by either man or spirit.

Shebbear is on a minor road between the A3072 and the A388, some 8 miles north-east of Holsworthy.

Nearest railway station: Exeter.

SOUTHEND-ON-SEA, Essex

Whitebait Festival

The festival that takes place here in early September celebrates the opening of the whitebait season in the kind of 'harvest home' of the sea that used to take place in many fishing communities all over Britain. The first whitebait festival was held in Dagenham in the 1780s and was later transferred to Greenwich where it continued to be celebrated until pollution drove the fish from that part of the Thames; the custom was revived at Southend in 1934.

The first catch of whitebait – young herrings or mackerel – is blessed by the Archdeacon of Southend and is then served at a banquet attended by the Lord Mayor of London, cabinet ministers and the Fishmongers' Guild.

Southend-on-Sea, part of the great conurbation on the northern shore of the Thames estuary, is reached by the A13 from London.

Nearest railway station: Southend-on-Sea.

TATWORTH, Somerset

Candle Auction

A candle auction takes place every year here on the first Tuesday after 6 April, Old Lady Day. About twenty-five people, who together constitute Stowell Court, meet to take part in auctioning a piece of land called Stowell Mead, which includes a watercress bed, and also to share a supper of bread, cheese and watercress. A tallow candle is used and the last bid made before it burns out secures the use of the mead for a year. The village lies on a minor road about 2 miles to the south of Chard.

Nearest railway stations: Axminster, Taunton.

TICHBORNE, Hampshire

Tichborne Dole

This dole, which is annually distributed on 25 March to the parishioners of Tichborne, Cheriton and Lane End, is one of the oldest charities in England. According to the tradition handed down in the Tichborne family, it was founded in the twelfth century by Lady Maybella, wife of Sir Roger de Tichborne. In her lifetime she was extremely generous to the local poor, and when she was dying she tried to ensure that they would not suffer by her death. She asked her husband to provide an annual dole of bread on Lady Day. He, taking a burning brand from the fire, told her that he would give as much land for this purpose as she could walk round before the flame went out. In view of her weak state, this practically amounted to a refusal of her request, and no doubt it was so intended. But Lady Maybella was not to be thus easily defeated. She ordered her women to carry her outside and then, finding she could not walk, she began to crawl over the ground as rapidly as she could. In this way she managed to cover an astonishing 23 acres of land, still known as the Crawls, before the torch flickered out. Before she died, she made her husband promise to honour his bargain; in addition, she warned him that if he or any of his descendants stopped the dole so hardly won, a curse would fall on the family. Their fortunes would fail, their name would be changed, the house would fall down and the ancient line would die out. As a sign of this, there would be a generation of seven sons followed by one of seven daughters; then the end would come.

The dole was duly given without interruption until 1796, when it was stopped and the revenues of the Crawls were diverted by Sir Henry Tichborne to the church. In due course, Sir Henry had seven sons, his heir had seven daughters and part of the house collapsed. These rather alarming coincidences gave the family pause for thought. The dole was restored by Sir Edward Doughty-Tichborne and since then it has been distributed with unfailing regularity each year.

In 1948, however, it was seriously endangered through no fault of the Tichbornes. Bread rationing was still in operation, and the Ministry of Food refused to issue the necessary bread coupons for the dole. This was reported in almost every newspaper, with full accounts of the curse that threatened the family if they were to fail in their duty. As a result, more than 5000 bread coupons were received from people all over the country. Strictly speaking this was illegal, as the Ministry pointed out; public opinion, however, was on the family's side and finally officialdom gave way.

In its present form, the dole consists not of loaves, but of a ton and a half of flour made from wheat grown on the Crawls. An open-air service is held, which is conducted either by the Tichbornes' chaplain or by the Roman Catholic Bishop of Portsmouth. Prayers are offered for the repose of Lady Maybella's soul and the flour is blessed and distributed to the villagers. A gallon is given to every male applicant and, somewhat unfairly, half a gallon to each woman and child.

The village is about 1 mile off the A31, reached from a turning to the south some 6 miles east of Winchester. It is famed not only for its dole, but for the notorious 'Tichborne Claimant' case of the 1870s, and for the tomb of a Tichborne infant, supposedly cursed to death by a gypsy in the fifteenth century.

Nearest railway station: Winchester.

TISSINGTON, Derbyshire

Well-dressing
Springs and wells have always been venerated, from exceedingly remote times onwards, because water is a basic necessity of life and to our forefathers it seemed a mysterious and spirit-haunted thing. A lively spring which brought fertility to the land where it flowed, and to the men and beasts who depended upon that land, was once almost universally supposed to be the dwelling place of some powerful spirit to whom prayer and sacrifice were due. Wells were thus honoured with religious ceremonies and dances, and decorated with flowers and green branches at the greater festivals. When Christianity came, water-worship as such was strictly forbidden, but most of the ancient and well-loved springs were purged of their pagan associations, purified and rededicated to the Blessed

Virgin Mary or to one of the saints. The wells were still dressed with flowers and honoured with processions and similar rites on great feast days, but now it was done for the glory of God, and in thanksgiving for the gift of water, and no longer in praise of, or to placate any indwelling spirit.

Well-dressing in Derbyshire is a relic of this ancient form of worship, though in no part of that county has it continued uninterrupted since pagan times. On the contrary, it has always been a very intermittent custom and even the most famous of all the dressings, that at Tissington, is only supposed to run back as far as 1350. It comes and it goes, like the land springs in the chalk hills of southern England. But a lapse is frequently followed by a revival, and no one can safely predict in what village the ritual will suddenly restart after a very long pause. In form it has changed considerably in the last 150 years and it has now become an intricate and beautiful craft which does not appear to be known elsewhere.

Until the beginning of the nineteenth century the wells seem to have been decorated with simple garlands, but by about 1818, boards 'cut to the figure intended to be represented, and covered with moist clay' began to appear. The modern well-dressing consists normally of a large picture, usually religious in subject, and made from a mosaic of overlapping flower petals (or in some villages flower heads tightly packed together), leaves, berries, tree cones, bark, mosses and lichens, pressed upon a wooden background covered with soft clay. Everything used in the picture has to be of natural origin. Pebbles or fine quartz, sand or small shells may be included, but not pieces of glass or tin or any other manufactured material. The clay has to be dampened with water and salt, kneaded, rolled and well worked by hand, and then laid, thickly and very smoothly upon the wooden screen.

The chosen design is transferred to it either by being drawn directly on it – if there is a capable artist available – with a sharp-pointed instrument or, more usually, by making a full-size copy on paper, laying it upon the clay surface and pricking it through with a skewer. All this, together with the arduous task of collecting together the necessary flowers and other materials, the making of the picture itself and finally the careful erection of the finished product behind the well for which it was designed, is in the hands of the local men. Many of them have been well-dressing for years and some can claim to have had a father or a grandfather who was himself an experienced worker in this beautiful rural craft.

Of the various places in Derbyshire where well-dressing is or was customary, Tissington has the longest tradition. One account says that the custom began there in 1615 after a severe drought lasting from March until September. Alone in the district Tissington's five wells continued to flow without ceasing throughout that dreadful time, supplying not only their own people but also many men and animals who came from outlying communities. Thereafter, the well-dressing was observed as a form of thanksgiving. Another story, however, says that it began in 1350 because, during the Black Death of 1348–9, when hundreds of Derbyshire people perished from the plague, Tissington remained untouched because, it was said, of the purity of its water.

Possibly both these tales are true and all that was done in 1615 was to revive an ancient ceremony that had been allowed to lapse. It now takes place annually on Ascension Day, beginning with a service of thanksgiving in the church; afterwards a procession of clergy, choir and congregation goes to bless each of the five wells – Yewtree Well, Hall Well, Hands Well, Coffin Well and Town Well.

Tissington is a village of great beauty at the southern end of the Peak District National Park, about 4 miles from Ashbourne; take the A515 road north from that town, and turn east down a side road a mile or so beyond Fenny Bentley.

Nearest railway stations: Derby, Uttoxeter.

TWYFORD, Hampshire

Bellringers' Feast

The annual feast given to the bellringers on 7 October in this pretty village just south of Winchester commemorates the narrow escape of a local landowner, William Davis, who heard the church bells ringing and changed direction just in time to save himself from falling into a deep chalk pit. In his will, dated 1754, he provided for the annual pealing of the bells on the anniversary of this adventure, and for a subsequent feast for the ringers, in which the whole village participates.

Nearest railway station: Winchester.

WARCOP, Cumbria

Rush-bearing

Rush-bearing ceremonies have become garland-bearing festivals at Warcop and its neighbouring village of Great Mus-grave. In both places there is a procession of little girls wearing on their heads flower crowns made of light wood covered entirely with blossom. They are traditional – garland headdresses of this kind were worn during the last century, when the festival was really concerned with rush-strewing in the church. There are no rushes now, although about forty years ago the vicar of Warcop arranged for boys to carry rush crosses in the procession, which takes place on 29 June, to remind people of the real meaning of the celebration. (For more about the origins of rush-bearing, see *Grasmere*, page 32.)

Warcop and Great Musgrave are about 20 miles east and slightly north of Grasmere. Leave the M5 motorway at junction 38 and drive east along the A685 to Kirkby Stephen; follow the B6259 road north from Kirkby Stephen for about 4 miles – Great Musgrave is down a side road going east and Warcop is a couple of miles further up the B6259.

Nearest railway station: Appleby.

WEST WITTON, North Yorkshire

Burning of Bartle

The custom known as the Burning of Bartle is observed in West Witton on a Saturday near St Bartholomew's Day, 24 August. Formerly the ceremony took place on St Bartholomew's Day itself, which is the patronal festival of the parish and was at one time the beginning of a week-long feast and holiday. The transfer to a varying Saturday date is a matter of modern convenience.

A large effigy, usually more than lifesize, is carried in procession round the village. If any car or bus is encountered on the way, Bartle is lifted up to the windows so that the passengers may see him. Similarly if any house door is left open, the procession halts outside it, the effigy is displayed to those within, and the following rhyme is declaimed by one of the bearers:

At Penn Hill crags he tore his rags,
At Hunter's Thorn he blew his horn,
At Capplebank Stee he brak his knee,
At Grassgill Beck he brak his neck,
At Waddam's End he couldn't fend,
At Grassgill End he made his end.

In another recorded version of this ditty, the place name Briskill is given instead of Grassgill but whichever is correct, it is at the bottom of Grassgill that Bartle now makes his end. When that point is reached, he is soaked in paraffin and thrown on to a large bonfire. There he burns while hidden fireworks explode all round him and the watching crowds cheer, shout and sing the popular songs of the moment at the tops of their voices.

Who or what Bartle represents is uncertain. His name and the date both suggest that he is Saint Bartholomew and according to Edmund Bogg, who wrote in the 1890s, that is whom he was then supposed to be. But nothing in the history of the great saint and apostle provides any reason for such a celebration, and although the custom is sometimes vaguely associated with the Massacre of St Bartholomew's Day in 1572, the local legends of Bartle himself have no ecclesiastical or saintly connections. One legend is that Bartle was a robber who, at some unspecified period, raided the swinepens of the district and was eventually captured on Penn Hill. Another says he was a cattle-stealing giant killed by a band of

farmers. A third theory is that he was not mortal at all but a spirit of the forest that once stretched from Middleham to Bainbridge, and that he was associated with fertility and the harvest. The fact that the modern effigy evidently has some luck-bringing qualitites, as shown by the displays to passers-by and householders, may have some bearing on the last explanation. If so, it is possible that Bartle began life as some sort of harvest deity, to whom Saint Bartholomew's name was subsequently given because of the coincidence of dates.

The village of West Witton lies in the wonderful Wensleydale countryside of North Yorkshire about 15 miles west of Bedale. Turn off the A1 a mile or so east of Bedale, on the A684; drive through Bedale staying on the A684 and heading west through Leyburn and Wensley. The village is about 4 miles beyond Wensley.

Nearest railway station: Northallerton.

WHALTON, Northumberland

Midsummer Fires

Midsummer Day – 24 June – is the Feast of the Nativity of Saint John the Baptist, that great saint who was the herald of Christ and whose festival, unlike those of other saints, commemorates his birth rather than his death and entry into Paradise. It falls only three days after the Summer Solstice, the day on which the sun reaches its highest glory and thereafter begins to decline. In the liturgical calendar, the birthday is equated with it.

In ancient times, the solstice was marked by a fire festival of great importance when, through countless centuries, the sun was ritually strengthened by bonfires burning everywhere on Midsummer Eve, by torchlight processions through the streets, by flaming tar barrels and, in some districts, by wheels bound with straw and tow, set alight and rolled down steep hillsides into the valley below.

All this was said in the Middle Ages to be performed in honour of Saint John, but in fact the fires were much older than he. If in pre-Christian times they were lit to give magical aid to the sun, which now, in the full tide of summer, began to wane, they were also lit, then as later, to bring fertility and prosperity to men, crops and herds.

In the Northumberland village of Whalton the change in the calendar which took place in 1752 has been ignored and the local people hold their time-honoured ceremony on 4 July, Old Midsummer Eve. It is called the Whalton Bale, when a great fire is lit on the village green and those who arrive to spectate dance around it, as of old. There is also sword dancing and Morris dancing to the music of fiddlers and Northumbrian pipers. 'Bale' derives from the Anglo-Saxon 'bael', meaning a great fire.

Whalton is little more than 10 miles to the north-west of Newcastle; take the A696 road to Belsay, then turn west on B6524. The village is about 2 miles down that road.

Nearest railway station: Morpeth.

Some of Cornwall's ancient bonfires have come to life again since the Federation of Old Cornwall Societies revived them between the two world wars of this century, and now a chain of fires is to be seen again on the Cornish hills at midsummer.

WHITBY, North Yorkshire

Planting the Penny Hedge

The Penny Hedge, or Horngarth, is planted annually on the morning of Ascension Eve below high-tide mark on the river shore at Boyes Staith, Whitby. This is an ancient tenure custom whereby certain lands were formerly held from the abbots of Whitby by the service of erecting a stout fence, or hedge, made of stakes and interlaced osiers. It had to be strong enough to withstand the force of three tides, and to be in position by nine o'clock on the appointed morning, unless the state of the tide made this impossible. Other conditions had also to be fulfilled and these too are still in force today.

The age of this service is unknown, but it is certainly very old and may possibly run back to Saxon times. A local legend fixed its origins in the middle of the twelfth century and connects it with a penance. According to this tale, William de Bruse (or Bruce), Ralph de Percy and a freeholder named Allatson went hunting on 16 October 1159 in the woods of Eskdale-side. These woods were on the Abbot of Whitby's lands and in them was a hermitage where one of the monks of the abbey was then living. The three huntsmen started a wild boar which fled before their hounds and, when nearly exhausted, ran for shelter into the chapel of the hermitage. The hermit, either from a desire to save the boar – which died almost immediately – or simply to save the chapel from being overrun, shut the door in the faces of the hounds. When their owners arrived, they found the frustrated pack milling about and baying outside. In their rage at this interruption of their sport, they beat the hermit so unmercifully that he died soon afterwards though, luckily for them, not before he was able to save them from their well-merited punishment.

Not only did he forgive them for his sufferings and death but he also persuaded the infuriated abbot, who was demanding the full penalties for murder and sacrilege, to be satisfied with the penance which the hermit himself devised. This was that they and their descendants should henceforth hold their land from the abbot and his successors by the service of the Horngarth. They were required to go every year at sunrise on Ascension Eve to Stray-head Wood, where the abbot's bailiff awaited them, and there to cut a prescribed number of stakes and osiers with a knife valued at 'one penny' hence the name of the custom. Such a cheap, small knife, of course, made the cutting of stakes hard work. They were to carry these stakes upon their backs through Whitby to a point on the river shore before 9.00 a.m. If it was then full tide they need do no more; if not, they were to set about building their strong hedge. At intervals during the work, and when it was completed, the bailiff was to sound his horn and cry 'Out upon ye! Out upon ye!' as a reminder of their dreadful crime. If this service was refused at any time, the holding was forfeit.

That service is rendered now for part of the original lands to the lord of the manor of Whitby. The tenant, usually surrounded by an admiring crowd, drives his stakes into the muddy ground and joins them with the osiers to make a stout, tide-resisting hedge of the age-old pattern. The manor bailiff stands by and when the work is finished, blows a blast on an ancient horn and cries 'Out ye! Out ye!' as his ecclesiastical predecessor did of old. It is his duty to see also that the tenant builds the Horngarth strong enough to withstand three successive tides. In another sense the Horngarth has withstood the passage of eight centuries – and possibly more.

The harbour town of Whitby stands on the rugged coast about 20 miles north of Scarborough. Follow the A64 road from York towards Scarborough, then take the A171 up the coast; or turn north off the A64 and on to the A169 near Malton, driving up through Pickering and over the North Yorkshire Moors.

Nearest railway station: Whitby.

WINCHESTER, Hampshire

Wayfarer's Dole

This ancient charity which is given daily at the Hospital of St Cross, near Winchester, has been in existence since the twelfth century when, in 1136, Henry de Blois founded the hospital as a home for thirteen poor men. In 1446 Cardinal Beaufort added another almshouse, that of 'Noble Poverty' for men of higher rank who had fallen on evil days through no fault of their own. Both these foundations exist today as separate institutions under one head. The two sets of beneficiaries are still distinguished by their picturesque gowns; the Blois Brethren, the original poor men, wear black gowns and the silver cross of the Knights Hospitallers of St John, and the Beaufort Brethren wear dark red and the Cardinal's hat-badge. All enjoy free housing and allowances for food, and pocket money.

In Henry de Blois's time, the hospital provided free meals for 100 poor people every day; later the number was increased to 200. This open-handed generosity declined at one period, during which incompetent or corrupt Masters of the Hospital allowed the revenues to be deflected, but matters were put right in the fifteenth century by William of Wykeham. Nevertheless, in good or evil times, charity never ceased to be dispensed here in some measure. The Wayfarers' Dole is still given every day to the first thirty-two persons who come to the porter's lodge to ask for it. It consists of a piece of white bread which is handed to the traveller on an old carved wooden platter, and a draught of ale served in a horn bearing the arms of the order. No questions are asked, and no conditions have to be fulfilled by the applicant; the only distinction ever made is that those who are really in need receive much larger portions.

Nearest railway station: Winchester.

WIRKSWORTH, Derbyshire

Queen of the Wells

At a number of Derbyshire towns and villages, ancient well-dressing ceremonies were transferred to public taps when water was first laid on. At Wirksworth this happened in 1840 but today the taps have all disappeared. However, the very fine well-dressings are set up in Whit week, on traditional but now waterless sites. There is a Queen of the Wells and a festival which is one of the highlights of the year in this small town of narrow streets and stone houses, where George Eliot set much of her novel *Adam Bede*. It lies 5 miles south of Matlock; take the A6 road through Matlock Bath and turn on to the B5023 at Cromford.

Nearest railways tations: Cromford, Matlock.

For more information about Derbyshire well-dressing ceremonies, see *Tissington*, page 82.

WORKINGTON, Cumbria

Street Football

Football of the old, wild type, with no definite rules and teams of indeterminate size, was one of the traditional sports of Shrovetide. It was, of course, played at other times, not only at high festivals such as Christmas and Easter but also quite commonly on Sundays and local holidays. At Workington it still exists as a vigorous street game played out between teams known as the Uppies and Downies on Good Friday, Easter Tuesday and the Saturday following. There are two goals, one at the harbour and the other a mile away by the park wall surrounding ruined Workington Hall. Once, the rival teams were made up of coal miners and dock workers, but the battle is now between folk of the Upper Town and Lower Town. Hundreds of men – not to mention women! – join in on each side.

The mining and steel town is at the mouth of the Solway Firth, just a few miles north of Whitehaven on the A595 road.

Nearest railway station: Workington.

WOTTON, Surrey

Forty Shilling Day

In 1717 William Glanville of this North Downs village provided in his will for the payment of forty shillings each, to five poor boys, aged sixteen or less, who fulfilled the conditions that he laid down. On the anniversary of his death, whenever that should occur, they were to go to his tomb, lay their hands upon it and recite from memory the Lord's Prayer, the Apostle's Creed and the Ten Commandments. They were also to read aloud the First Epistle of Saint Paul to the Corinthians and write two verses of the same chapter in a clear and legible hand. This curious bequest is still honoured in full – though perhaps more for the fun of participating than for the cash – on what is now locally known as Forty Shilling Day. This should be, and usually is, 2 February, the anniversary of the day on which William Glanville died. But since his tomb is in the churchyard, the ceremony is sometimes postponed if the weather is exceptionally unpleasant. The vicar of Wotton selects the beneficiaries amongst local choirboys and schoolboys.

Wotton lies a little to the west of Dorking, on the A25.

Nearest railway station: Dorking.

YARNTON, Oxfordshire

Lot Meadow Mowing

The custom known as Lot Meadow Mowing is an ancient method of apportioning strips of grassland which is still in use at Yarnton, as it has been for centuries. Two meadows called West Mead and Pixey Mead are divided into lot-strips of varying size, and once a year lots are drawn for them by freeholders of Yarnton, Wolvercote and Begbroke who own the mowing rights.

The owners of the mowing rights may, if they wish, sell their hay in advance and for this purpose an auction is held at the Grapes Inn on the Monday after St Peter's Day (29 June) or as near to it as the state of the crop permits. In the following week, on a day fixed by the Head Meadsman, who is in charge of the proceedings, the lessees, or those who have bought the hay from them, go to the meadows where they are met by the Meadsmen. All the strips are marked with stakes, with the exception of the Tydals which are marked with stones. These are the portions that have been permanently assigned to the rectories of Yarnton and Begbroke in lieu of tithes.

The Head Meadsman carries a bag containing thirteen very old wooden balls, known as Mead Balls. On each there is a name – Gilbert, Harry, White, Boat, William, Rothe, Walter Jeoffrey, Freeman, Green, Dunn, Perry, Boulton and Watery Molly. Each ball represents a certain acreage, reckoned by a system of measurement in which the term 'a man's mowth', that is, as much as a man can mow in a single day, is used.

The drawing begins at 8.00 a.m. For each lot, or part of a lot, a ball is drawn from the bag. Some of the grass is then cut with a few sweeps of the scythe and the initials of the man to whom the lot has fallen are cut on the ground. This process is repeated until all the strips have been apportioned and the boundaries between them marked out by – nowadays – a tractor. Then mowing begins.

Until the beginning of the last century, it was customary to mow each meadow in a single day and to celebrate the end of the work by general merrymaking. In order to keep to the one-day timetable labourers from elsewhere had to be employed; in some years a hundred or more poured into the village, as well as idlers who came to drink and amuse themselves. Fights became common and finally in 1817, after a man had been killed in a riot, the mowing time for each meadow was extended to three days, thereby eliminating the need for outside helpers and reducing the size of the crowds.

Today, the Lot Meadow Mowing is a matter of straight farming business without any general holiday associations. Nevertheless it is an interesting survival; it can be seen by taking the A34 north from Oxford on the appropriate day, then taking the left turning to Yarnton about 1 mile north-west of the junction with the A40.

Nearest railway station: Oxford.

YOULGREAVE, Derbyshire

Well-dressing

On the Saturday nearest St John the Baptist's Day (24 June), well-dressing ceremonies (see page 82) take place at the five old public taps in the ancient hilltop village of Youlgreave, on the edge of Bradford Dale. The village is set in magnificent limestone scenery about 3 miles to the south of Bakewell. Take the A6 south from Bakewell, turn right onto the B5056, and right again for Youlgreave.

Nearest railway station: Matlock.

WALES

NORTH AND SOUTH

Bardic Triumph

The Royal National Eisteddfod of Wales, the major event in the Welsh calendar, is held in north and south Wales in alternate years and in different sites, though there are plans to find the event a permanent home. It has existed in its present form since 1451 at least and has been established as an annual event since the end of the eighteenth century. Its principal function is to foster Welsh arts – poetry, music, dancing and crafts – and the proceedings are enacted entirely in Welsh.

Each eisteddfod really begins a year and a day before its first event takes place. Then the Arch Druid, wearing a chaplet of oak leaves and a copper breastplate, proclaims the next year's festival from the Arch Druid's stone in the middle of a specially built stone circle. When he has finished the inaugural speech, the Sword of Peace is laid before him. He raises it high and cries three times in Welsh 'Is it peace?' Each time the voice of the great crowd thunders back 'Heddwch!' (Peace.) The high point of the festival itself, which takes place in the first full week of the following August, is the crowning and chairing of the Bard, when the author of the winning poem is presented with the Bardic Crown, the greatest honour that a Welsh poet can receive. So high are the judges' standards that there have been several years when they have refused to award the prize at all rather than give it for a work they considered unworthy of the honour.

ANGLESEY, Gwynedd

The Egg-clappers

Anglesey children 'clap for eggs' at Eastertime, a custom that now seems to survive only in that island though formerly it existed in many other parts of north Wales. The children go round the farms and houses of the district carrying wooden clappers or, more usually now, two pieces of slate with which they make a noise like the rattle of castanets. They also sing a pathetic little ditty in Welsh, of which the English translation is 'Clap, clap, ask for an egg for the little boys of the parish.' Their object is, of course, to collect eggs, either for eating or for use in games. Anything else, however, is equally acceptable and here, as in other areas of Britain, the children are often given sweets, cakes or money by people who have not the time or the inclination to prepare the Pace Eggs of tradition (see *Midgley*, page 63).

Nearest railway stations: Bangor, Holyhead.

CARDIGAN, Dyfed

Barley Saturday

A vigorous survivor of the great horse

fairs that flourished all over Britain up to the end of the last century, Barley Saturday at Cardigan attracts visitors by the thousand to this ancient, bustling town at the mouth of the Teifi River in west Wales.

The event had its origins in the smaller town of Newcastle Emlyn, 10 miles further up the river, where traditionally a stallion fair was held on the last Friday in April. It was also at this time of year that farmworkers in the whole area around Cardigan enjoyed a brief rest from their labours after sowing the barley fields. They had wages accumulated since the hiring fair held in the November of the preceding year and would congregate in Cardigan for the Barley Fair held on the last Saturday in April. So it became the custom for farmers and pony and horse breeders to take their stallions down to Cardigan on the day following the Newcastle Emlyn fair.

In Cardigan mares and their owners would await the arrival of the stallions and many a bargain was struck in the courtyard of a local inn or pub, often cemented by the mare being covered there and then. Thus, some centuries ago, the Barley Fair – Dydd Sadwrn Barlys, as it is called in Welsh – evolved into an event of great importance to breeders, not only in west Wales, but over the whole principality. It takes place still on the last Saturday in April (though in 1982 it was held on Saturday 1 May) and has come to be called simply Barley Saturday.

The festivities start with the stallion show, which draws entries from all the traditional breeds – cobs, ponies and shires – not to mention the best of local hunters. They parade through the thronged, narrow streets of the town, after which the class winners are pre-sented with their trophies before setting off on another triumphal parade down Pendre Street. This time they are followed by a grand procession of vintage and veteran traction engines, steam-rollers, tractors and cars – chuffing, clanking, rattling tributes to the loving care lavished on them by their owners.

Merrymaking continues all day in the town, where many of the old inns and pubs have changed little since the nineteenth century, when Cardigan was a busy seaport packed with sailing ships loading grain or slate from the great Welsh quarries inland.

Cardigan is approached from the north by the A487 road from Aberystwyth and from the east along the A484 through Newcastle Emlyn, where the stallion fair has, alas, been allowed to lapse. There are car parks in Quay Street, Bathhouse, Feidirfair and behind the Guildhall. The nearest railway station is 30 miles away in Carmarthen, from where a regular bus service operates to Cardigan.

CILGERRAN, Dyfed

Coracles of Teifi

Coracle Week, an event that takes place at Cilgerran each year in mid-August, provides one of the most unusual and exciting spectacles to be seen in west Wales. The village, which stands beside the strong but smoothly flowing River Teifi, has longed been famed for its salmon fishing, which is carried out in a manner that can hardly have changed since the days of the pre-Roman Celts. The salmon are netted, each end of the net being held by a man in a coracle, an efficient, light craft of ancient design that varies slightly in different parts of Wales. Teifi coracles consist of a light wicker frame over which calico is stretched then waterproofed with pitch; they are so light that a fisherman can easily carry one by himself.

Once a year these working craft have a gala of their own, when on the Saturday of the festival coracle races are held. The most important of these are the races between the Teifi coracles and those from the nearby River Towy, whose design is slightly different. There are also a number of other events, including ladies' and children's races and a coracle 'polo' match. For the visitor, perhaps the greatest joy is to see the speed and manoeuvrability achieved by these craft when they are paddled by skilled hands.

Cilgerran, loomed over by its great eleventh-century castle, lies on a minor road off the A478, some 2 miles south of Cardigan.

Nearest railway station: Carmarthen.

LAUGHARNE, Dyfed

Common Walk

Laugharne, the home and burial place of Dylan Thomas and said to have been the inspiration of *Under Milk Wood*, is governed under the terms of a charter that was granted to Guy de Brian in 1307. The ancient rights and privileges contained in the charter are guarded by the Court Leet and the Court Baron that meet on alternate Mondays, both presided over by an official known as the Portreeve.

One of the provisions in the charter concerns the confirmation of certain land tenures to seventy-six senior burgesses. These rights are granted and maintained by a Common Walk, a very old custom that is re-enacted every three years on Whit Monday – in 1984,

1987 and so on. Proceedings begin at 5.00 a.m., when the bailiff rings the Town Hall bell and a procession forms, consisting of the Portreeve, halberdmen, the Common Attorney, the Grand Jury and the burgesses eligible for the land tenures. These must be men over the age of twenty-one who are also the sons or sons-in-law of burgesses. When everyone is assembled the Common Walk begins, a perambulation of 24 miles over a course long-established by tradition. Halts are made at 'hoisting places' where the bounds are beaten and, understandably, refreshments are taken.

Laugharne is beautifully situated on the Taf estuary some 12 miles southwest of Carmarthen.

Nearest railway station: Carmarthen.

LLANGOLLEN, Clwd

Peace Through Music

The International Music Eisteddfod was founded here shortly after the Second World War with the aim of uniting all the peoples of the world through music – an aim that is summarized in the festival's motto, 'Happy is a world that sings, gentle are its songs.' It was a success from the start and now its participants are numbered in thousands, coming from as many as thirty countries, while perhaps a quarter of a million spectators may gather to applaud the sight and sound of the folk dancers and singers, most of whom are dressed in the national costumes of their homelands.

The eisteddfod, which is held in the second week of July, presents a programme of great brilliance and complexity that includes singing and instrumental competitions, dancing and choral performances, as well as special entertainments given by world-famous ballet companies or operatic groups. Details are usually printed in June and may be obtained by applying to the Secretary of the International Music Eisteddfod in Llangollen. Parking is of course at a premium during the festivities but if you are coming by car from England, the best way is probably via the A5 from Shrewsbury.

Nearest railway station: Ruabon.

LLANRHAEADR-YM-MOCHNANT, Clwd

Christmas in Wales

This and other villages in the Tanad Valley and Berwyn Mountains still keep up the old custom of the *plygeiniau*, a type of Christmas carol service that used to be held all over Wales. It consists of male-voice choirs who, in the Christmas season, wander through the area from church to church giving unaccompanied performances of carols in the Welsh language.

Llanrhaeadr-ym-Mochnant, famed chiefly for the nearby falls of Pistyll Rhaedr – one of the traditional Seven Wonders of Wales – is situated on the B4580 some 10 miles south-west of Oswestry.

Nearest railway station: Gobowen.

PENCOED, Glamorgan

The Mari Lwyd

Just as in England the Hodening Horse went round at Christmas or at Hallowtide, so in Wales his near kinsman the Mari Lwyd does the same between Christmas and Twelfth Night.

A horse skull is decorated with coloured ribbons and draped with a long white sheet on which two pieces of black cloth are sewn to represent the horse's ears. The skull has a spring in the lower jaw to enable the mouth to open and shut, and eye sockets filled with thick bottle glass. A pole is fixed to the underside and on this it is carried about by a man whose body is almost completely covered by a white sheet, so that only his feet are visible. A pair of reins with little bells attached to them is fixed to the skull; with these the Mari Lwyd is led or driven by his (or her) attendants.

Traditionally the latter consisted of five or six men and boys who wore coloured ribbons and rosettes stitched to their clothes, and sometimes a broad sash tied around the waist. The leader held the Mari Lwyd's reins and also a stick for knocking upon doors. The little group, with its awe-inspiring central figure, started out at dusk. On arrival at a house, the leader knocked on the door and, without waiting for it to be opened, asked 'permission to sing'. Then began a contest of rhymes and songs, some traditional and others made up on the spot. When 'permission to sing' had been requested, the inmates of the house inquired in verse how many stood outside and what their names were. The reply was also in verse, and this interchange often went on for a long time, both sides making up impromptu verses. Eventually, however, inspiration failed. If the householders were the first to stop singing or reciting, the door was opened and the visitors were admitted. If the Mari Lwyd party stopped first, they were supposed to go away and seek another; probably this was rarely allowed to happen since if they did not come in, half the fun of the evening was gone, and so was the good luck they brought.

Once inside, the Mari Lwyd ran about chasing and biting the women, while the leader pretended to restrain him, crying 'Whoa there!' and pulling on the reins. In Glamorgan, each member of the party had a special name and separate task, including Merryman, who played the fiddle and indulged in all sorts of antics; Judy, who carried a broom and swept the hearth; and Punch, who kissed the girls and was noisily chased by Judy with her broom.

This custom was once widespread throughout Wales and it still survives in Pencoed and other places in Glamorgan and Powys. In its present form it is not quite so elaborate as formerly; the men who go around with the skull are usually content with their ordinary dress and the different characters are not always clearly defined. The Mari Lwyd, however, is still the same mysterious figure, and if this ancient character as a bringer of fertility is largely forgotten, his visits are still associated with good luck and merriment. The name Mari Lwyd is usually said to mean 'Grey Mare' or 'Grey Mary', but no one seems to be really certain.

Pencoed is situated near exit 35 on the M4, a mile or so east of Bridgend.
Nearest railway station: Bridgend.

TENBY, Dyfed

Raindrops for Luck

This attractive and ancient town built on a rocky promontory overlooking Carmarthen Bay is the setting for a custom that may well predate Christianity. On New Year's Day the children of the town sprinkle passers-by with raindrops collected on sprigs of box or holly. Rather surprisingly it is considered lucky to be sprinkled in this way, and the children are rewarded with money or sweets. Very probably the practice was once part of a pre-Christian purification rite, but by the Middle Ages it had won the approval of the Church, and came to be associated with the Virgin Mary.

Another old rite is enacted in Tenby on 31 July each year, when the mayor and council open St Margaret's Fair by walking in procession round the thirteenth-century walls of the town.

Nearest railway station: Tenby.

SCOTLAND

BIGGAR, Strathclyde

New Year Fires

In Biggar on New Year's Eve there is still observed a custom that is a survival of the ancient and once very wide-spread practice of lighting communal bonfires at the Winter Solstice, the longest night of the year, which is 21 December, in order to drive out old evils and bring fertility to the crops and cattle in the year that is coming. At Biggar a huge bonfire containing many fireworks as well as fuel is slowly built up during the three or four weeks beforehand on a convenient piece of ground not far from where the Mercat Cross once stood. At about half-past nine on the night of 31 December a man specially chosen for the task sets light to the bonfire with a torch. Cheers greet the flames as they leap up, and for the next two and a half hours the night is filled with the sounds of crackling wood, snapping fireworks and general human rejoicing. Then, as midnight strikes, silence falls on the crowd, the church bells ring out and 'Auld Lang Syne' is sung by all present. Thereafter, a sort of Mischief Night begins and pranks of all kinds are played by young people of both sexes. Finally, men and boys go out first-footing – competing to be the first to cross the thresholds of their friends' houses in the New Year – until well into the small hours of the morning.

Biggar, on the A72 about 12 miles south-east of Lanark, was the home of Mary Fleming, one of the 'Four Marys', ladies-in-waiting to Mary Queen of Scots. She is remembered in the town each July at the Crowning of the Fleming Queen, when the prettiest girl in the district is crowned queen of the summer fair.

Nearest railway station: Carstairs.

BURGHEAD, Grampian

Burning the Clavie

The Burning of the Clavie is an ancient fire ritual, connected with the New Year, which is still annually performed at Burghead on 11 January (New Year's Eve Old Style). How old the custom is is uncertain, but some of its details show signs of very considerable age, with roots running backwards into pagan antiquity. Moreover, although the custom is now confined to Burghead, the evidence of various presbytery and kirk-session records of the seventeenth and eighteenth centuries show that something very like it once took place in several other East Coast fishing ports, and even as far inland as Inveravon, where according to seventeenth-century kirk records, flaming 'torches of firr' were carried 'superstitiouslie and Idolatrouslie' about the folds and fields at New Year.

On the afternoon of 11 January the Clavie is prepared according to certain time-honoured and inflexible rules by a band of young men whose leader is known as the Clavie King. Tradition demands that they should all be members of long-established local families. No stranger may take part in the work or handle the tools used. Everything needed for the construction of the Clavie must be given or borrowed; nothing must be bought, for that would be very unlucky. An Archangel tar barrel is sawn into two unequal parts. The upper and larger portion is broken up to serve as fuel later. The bottom half is fixed on to a salmon fisher's stake, about 6 or 8 feet in length and known as the Spoke, by means of a single long nail which has been specially forged for the purpose by the blacksmith. This nail has to be hammered in with a smooth, round stone, for the use of a metal hammer is strictly forbidden.

A herring cask is then broken up and its staves are fastened at 2-inch intervals round the bottom of the half-barrel, with their lower ends firmly fastened to the Spoke, leaving a space large enough to admit the head of the Clavie-bearer. The completed Clavie is propped against a wall and two young men standing on the latter fill it with dry, tar-soaked wood, piled up in the shape of a pyramid. At about 6.00 p.m. when everything is ready, the Clavie King sends one of his helpers to fetch a burning peat from a nearby house and with this, thrust into a hollow left for it in the pyramid, he sets the whole mass of fuel ablaze. Modern matches may not be used and the peat itself has to be already burning on the household fire before the messenger comes to receive it. Tar is poured over it, and with flames shooting high from its top the Clavie is raised aloft by the first of the bearers

amid loud cheers from the onlookers; then the procession starts on its way.

It goes all round the old town, following the old boundaries but leaving out the modern town which has grown up outside them. On the way, burning faggots are thrown from time to time for luck through the open doors of houses. To be the first to carry the Clavie is an honour, but no man could support the heat and the weight for long and so at certain points along the route, another takes on the burden. If the Clavie-bearer stumbled or fell it would be a very bad omen, both for the man himself and for the whole town.

Eventually, the procession arrives at a mound on the headland which is known as the Doorie Hill; here the Clavie comes to rest on an altar-like stone pillar with a socket in its top, into which the Spoke is fitted. Formerly a cairn of stones was prepared for it, but in 1809 the pillar was specially built for it, and this has been used ever since. As soon as the Clavie is in position, more wood is thrown onto it and fresh tar poured over, making the flames shoot up in a blaze that can be seen from a very long way off. Once the fire was kept burning all night with constant additions of wood and tar, but now it is allowed to burn only for a certain time, after which it is hacked to pieces by the Clavie King and his men. Burning fragments fly out in all directions, streams of flaming tar pour down the hill and everyone scrambles for bits of wood, regardless of scorched fingers. These embers, like the faggots thrown into the house doors, are luck-bringing and are treasured throughout the following year as a protection against evil, or are sent to Burghead men, or their descendants now living overseas.

The little fishing port of Burghead is on the enchanting Moray coast, on a minor road 8 miles west of Lossiemouth.

Nearest railway station: Forres.

COMRIE, Tayside

Flambeaux Procession

The little town of Comrie, which precisely straddles the line that divides Highlands from Lowlands, is on New Year's Eve the scene of a very colourful Flambeaux Procession, when men in strange and exotic costumes carry immense torches round the streets in a parade led by pipers and followed by a lively crowd, many of whom are in fancy dress. The procession starts from the square on the last stroke of midnight and there, after circuiting the town, it returns. The flambeaux, still alight, are thrown on the ground; round this pile people and flambeaux-bearers together dance until it is burnt out. Fire festivals of various kinds have been a way of celebrating New Year in Scotland since time immemorial.

Comrie lies by the A85, about 20 miles west of Perth.

Nearest railway station: Perth.

EDINBURGH

May Morning Dew

Gathering dew in the early hours of May Morning and washing one's face in it is a centuries-old custom which is often said to be forgotten now, but which in fact lingers on in a great many places. May Day is, of course, the occasion of several other folk rites and rituals. Young girls in country districts still go out before sunrise on May Day, alone or in little bands, to collect dew

from the grass and the bushes and anoint their faces with it. They do this because they believe as their ancestors did before them that it will make their complexions beautiful, or remove freckles and other blemishes; also the due performance of the rite is supposed to bring good luck in the following twelve months.

May dew is still valued as a beautifying and luck-bringing agent. Searching for it before dawn is of course mainly a country custom, but in Edinburgh, where the hills come close to the city, small parties of young people may still be seen walking through the King's Park by the Palace of Holyroodhouse to Arthur's seat – once a famous rendezvous for this purpose – there to wash their faces in the dew and to make a May-Day wish by St Anthony's Well.

INNERLEITHEN, Borders

Cleiking the De'il

Ronan was a disciple of St Columba and is said to have arrived in Scotland on the back of a sea monster; at any rate he came to Innerleithen, where the rivers of Tweed and Leithen meet, in AD 737 to do battle with the Devil and to drive him out by means of good works and the teaching of the Gospel. The saint's success is recalled by the sulphurous, and supposedly healing, waters of the well named after him, though until the beginning of the nineteenth century, it was simply called the Dow Well, from the Gaelic *dubh*, meaning black.

Ronan is also recalled in late July by the charming, week-long Cleikum Ceremonies, in which the Dux–head – boy of St Ronan's School represents the saint. Attended by the Dux Boys of each class, all dressed in monks' habits, he is officially proclaimed by the provost (mayor), and is given a crozier with which to 'cleik [smite] the De'il'. He then leads a torchlight procession to a cross in the churchyard where, after a service, he releases a flock of doves.

On the final evening of Cleikum Week, an effigy of the Devil is ceremoniously carried to the top of Caerlee Hill and is there solemnly burned in a great bonfire, so ensuring that the De'il has been well and truly cleiked – at least until the next July.

Innerleithen is on the A72 about 9 miles west of Galashiels.

There are no convenient railways stations: Edinburgh is nearest.

IRVINE, Strathclyde

Marymass Races

Marymass Fair, which is held here in the third week of August, dates from the twelfth century. The name of the fair links it to the parish church, which is dedicated to Our Lady. But ever since Mary Queen of Scots paid a visit to the town in 1563, the Marymass Queen – the girl chosen to preside over the festivities – has been dressed as Mary Stuart. A popular ingredient of the fair is the amateur horseracing, which includes a race for carthorses. It has been said that these races are of earlier origin than the fair itself, in which case this must be one of the oldest race meetings in the world.

Irvine, a port on the Firth of Clyde, is on the A71 about 7 miles west of Kilmarnock.

Nearest railway station: Irvine.

JEDBURGH, Borders

Jethart Ba'

This, the traditional handball game of Jedburgh, is played every year on Candlemas Day and again on Fastern's E'en. The date of the Candlemas Ba' is of course fixed on 2 February, but that of the Fastern's E'en, meaning the eve of the Lenten fast, is commonly applied to Shrove Tuesday throughout Lowland Scotland and the English northern counties. In Jedburgh, however, the anniversary is not reckoned by the normal ecclesiastical calendar, but by an old rhyme which says:

> First comes Candlemas,
> Then the new moon,
> The First Tuesday after
> Is aye Fastern's E'en.

Thus the second of Jedburgh's festival games may be played on Shrove Tuesday in some years, but in others it may take place on another date.

Jethart Ba' is a vigorous form of handball, played through the town streets between shop and house windows that have been carefully barricaded beforehand. It sometimes overflows into gardens and usually reaches the River Jed, where a great deal of splashing and ducking occurs. The balls used are decorated with coloured streamers and are thrown, run away with, 'smuggled' from hand to hand, but never kicked. Originally the game was a wild type of football; but in 1704 the town council forbade 'the tossing and throwing up of the football at Fastern's E'en within the streets of the burgh' because this had 'many times tended to the great prejudice of the inhabitants . . . there have been sometymes both old and young near lost their lives thereby'. Football having been thus prohibited, handball was, after an interval, substituted for it.

There are two sides, the Uppies, or

men born above the site of the Mercat Cross, who play towards the Castle Hill where they have their 'hail', and the Downies, or downwards men, who play towards the Townfoot. If of recent years it cannot be said that any have 'near lost their lives thereby', Jethart Ba' remains an extremely strenuous game which cheerfully disrupts the life of the town on both the days concerned. In 1849 the burgh authorities attempted to suppress it altogether by prohibiting the play and fining several of the most prominent players. But Jedburgh people were not to be so easily deprived of their traditional sport and appealing to the High Court of Edinburgh, they secured a ruling that the right to play the game in the streets of the town was sanctioned by immemorial usage.

A local legend says that the custom began in the days of border warfare when, after a fight at Ferniehurst Castle, the victorious Scots played football with the severed heads of their English enemies. This is a fine bloodthirsty tale, still half-believed in the district. In fact, ball games of various kinds have been played at Shrovetide from 'time out of mind', in England as well as in Scotland, and in the latter country also at Candlemas and on the variable Fastern's E'en observed in Jedburgh. Jethart Ba' is now perhaps the best-known of the northern celebrations because, as the official guide to the burgh proudly states; 'Alone among the towns of Scotland, Jedburgh continues to celebrate the coming of Candlemas by the playing of the ba'; and at Fastern's E'en, Jethart Ba' possesses pride of place among the contests annually played at various places on the Borders.'

Jedburgh, whose great abbey was gutted by the Earl of Surrey in 1523, is the very heart of the 'Debatable Lands'. It is on the A7, the road north from Carlisle and England.

There are no convenient railway stations: Newcastle is nearest.

LANARK, Strathclyde

Whuppity Stourie

Whuppity Stourie (or Scoorie) is an old springtime custom which is peculiar to the Royal Burgh of Lanark. It takes place on the first day of March and begins with the ringing of the town bell in the parish church. Between the beginning of October and the end of February this bell is not rung at six o'clock every evening as it is during the rest of the year, but on 1 March the nightly ringing begins again. Crowds of children come to the cross and wait outside the church, together with many adult spectators and the provost and other town officials, who watch the proceedings from a platform erected for their use. Each child carries a home-made weapon consisting of a tightly rolled ball of paper tied to the end of a long string. As soon as the bell's note is heard, they all rush off round the church, whirling their paper balls round their heads and beating each other with them as they run. They thus circuit the church three times and then there is a wild scramble for coins thrown to them from the platform; £10 is allotted annually for this purpose from one of the town funds. When the scramble is over, the provost addresses the assembled people, children and adults alike, with a few cheerful words and so the brief and lively celebration comes to its end for that year.

This is the modern form of Whuppity Stourie. The runners are now all children, but until at least as late as the first decade of the present century the youths of the town also took part. The customary weapons then were not paper balls but the caps, or bonnets, of the runners attached to cords. With these the lads not only beat each other but also attempted to strike the bell-ringer as they ran, a proceeding known as 'buffing the bell-man'. As soon as the church had been circuited thrice, they all dashed away to the Wellgate Head to meet the youths of New Lanark; a stand-up fight with the stringed bonnets followed. Afterwards the victors paraded the streets, their leader carrying a flag made from a handkerchief fixed on a pole and all loudly singing:

Hooray, boys, hooray!
For we have won the day.
We've met the bold New (Old) Lanark boys
And chased them doun the brae.

There is no fight now for this part of the proceedings was suppressed by the magistrates, but hearty blows with the paper balls are still exchanged as the children run round the church.

Various theories have been put forward to account for the whole curious ritual, of which the origin is very uncertain. One is that it is intended to herald or welcome the spring. Another explains it as a commemoration of a former custom of whipping penitents round the church. The latter theory would not cover the fight, which was probably the most important part of the whole affair for those who took part in it. It seems probable, in view of the springtime date, the ringing of bells and general noise, the former battle and the emphasis even now upon blows given and received, that here we have the remains of that ancient magical rite

– found in various forms in many northern countries – whereby winter and all its attendant evils was fought, defeated and finally driven away from the land.

Lanark and New Lanark, the splendid model town built by Robert Owen in 1784, lie some 10 miles south-east of Glasgow.

Nearest railway stations: Lanark and Carstairs.

LANGHOLM, Dumfries and Galloway

Common Riding

A number of Border towns – Selkirk, Hawick, Lauder, Sanquhar and Lockerbie among them, as well as Langholm – still recall the moss-trooping days of the Border raids in the annual Common Ridings. These seem to be partly an assertion of ancient rights and partly a statement of pride, to show that the hard-riding skills of the Border people in earlier centuries have not yet been dissipated.

Langholm, which lies only 8 miles from England, was the home, in the sixteenth century, of Johnnie Armstrong and the Armstrong clan, most notorious of the reivers or cattle-rustlers. Though now more famed for its tweed than for its raiders, the town still holds its Common Riding and fair each year at the end of July.

The celebrations begin when horsemen and horsewomen gather in the square and the provost – mayor – presents a banner to the person chosen as the Cornet for the year; the town crier then proclaims the people's rights to cut peat and bracken on the commons. The Cornet spurs his horse up a hillside and follows a tough course across the moors, followed by the other riders. The posse halts at various points to cut turf and pull swathes of bracken. Afterwards the riders progress through the town carrying traditional symbols – a wooden fish nailed to a plaque, a crown of plaited roses and a great thistle made of real thistles interwoven – representing the Union of the Crowns and ancient fishing rights.

The riders then return to the square, where the town crier announces:

So now I will conclude and say nae mair,
And if ye're pleased, I'll cry the Langholm Fair.

The burgh of Langholm is situated on the A7 about 18 miles north of Carlisle.
Nearest railway station: Carlisle.

LERWICK, Shetland

Up-Helly-Aa

The splendid fire festival of Up-Helly-Aa is held annually at Lerwick, traditionally on Twenty-Fourth Night (29 January) but now always on the last Tuesday in January. Twenty-Fourth Night is, or was, so called because it marked the end of the festivities of Yule (Old Style), which in this northern region lasted for twenty-four days.

Up-Helly-Aa has a long history of which perhaps not the least interesting detail is the manner in which the celebrations have blossomed and expanded during the last hundred years. Until as late as the 1870s the principal features of the day were not, as now, a torchlight procession and a burning ship but blazing tar barrels. These were dragged through the streets on wooden sledges by young men known as 'Guizers' or 'Disguisers'. Each sledge contained from four to eight barrels and was drawn by chains, whose rattling made a fine din to which the young men added by horn-blowing. This lively business continued through most of the night; and when it was over, the Guizers, clad in exotic costumes, went round the town visiting the houses of their friends and being warmly welcomed as luck-bringers until morning came.

These were time-honoured customs which can be traced a long way back. Fire and the visits of Guizers are still essentials of the festival in its modern form, but the tar barrels have gone. In 1874, the town authorities banned them because of the danger of fire, and also because housewives complained that tar spilt on the roads and brought in on the boots of their menfolk fouled their houses for days afterwards. But this prohibition did not bring the old Yule-end rejoicings to a close. The Guizers remained, and when a short time later a festival committee was formed, its leader was their elected chief, the Worthy Chief Guizer, now known as the Guizer Jarl. A torchlight procession was introduced in place of the tar barrels; in 1889, that procession was led for the first time by the dragon-headed model of a Norse galley which has been the main glory of the celebration ever since.

Preparations for Up-Helly-Aa go on for months beforehand. The 31-foot galley, with its oars and heraldic shields, has to be built and decorated, and some seven or eight hundred torches made from wood and sacking. The Guizers split up into squads, each squad representing a special theme of its members' own choosing and designing costumes to correspond. Themes and costumes are both kept strictly secret from all but the Guizer Jarl until the actual day of the festival. There is also 'The Bill', or 'Guizer Jarl's Proclamation', which appears on Up-Helly-Aa morning displayed upon a 10-feet-high decorated board set up at the Mercat Cross. 'The Bill' is a lively document, full of satirical references to local institutions and personages and humorous accounts of the events of the past year. It is quite modern, having been introduced as recently as 1931, but it is extremely popular and an example of how customs can evolve over the years. People from all over Lerwick flock to read it as soon as it is visible.

At a little before 7.00 p. m. the Norse galley is brought to the starting point of the procession and the torch-bearers take up their appointed places along the route behind it. The Guizer Jarl, in full Viking armour and flowing cloak, takes his place at the helm, with his own squad of Guizers, also dressed as Vikings, lined up alongside the ship. At half-past seven, the double ranks of paraffin-soaked torches are lit by flares and the procession moves briskly off to the singing of 'The Up-Helly-Aa Song'. Bands play, the different squads of Guizers march in their order through the streets bright with torch fire, and ahead of all goes the Norse longship carrying its memories of the 600 years when the Shetlands and the Orkneys were both subject to the Norse crown. When the Burning Site is finally reached, the torch-bearers form a huge fiery ring round the galley; the Guizer Jarl leaves it and at the sound of a bugle, all the torches are flung into the ship, which at once bursts into flames. While it burns 'The Norseman's Home' is sung, ships in the harbour sound their sirens and a great cheer goes up from the watching crowds. In less than an hour the galley is totally consumed and nothing remains but ashes.

This is not, however, the end of the proceedings. After the burning, the Guizers go round the town as of old, though they no longer visit private houses. Instead each squad, in turn and in strict order, visits every one of the thirteen halls of Lerwick, where refreshments and entertainments are organized for them by local hostesses and where they dance and make merry and usually give some sort of performance based upon their own special theme. As there are about fifty of these squads, this takes time, but nobody minds. Revelry and general merriment continue unabated all through the night and not until daylight pallidly appears at about six or seven o'clock is Up-Helly-Aa, and with it the final festivities of Yule, truly ended for that year.

Lerwick is not the easiest place to get to, especially in January. There are ferries from Aberdeen and Scrabster, but it is probably best to go by air from Aberdeen.

QUEENSFERRY, Lothian

Burryman's Blessing

On the day before the Ferry Fair at Queensferry, the Burryman perambulates the town visiting the houses and receiving cheerful greetings and gifts of money from the householders. No one knows how or when this custom began, but it is obviously much older than the fair with which it is now associated. The latter is not very old as fairs go, dating only from 1687; it was originally held on Saint James's Day, 25 July, and now takes place in the second week of August.

The Burryman needs to be of robust

physique because his annual task is an arduous one. He is dressed from head to foot in white flannel so closely covered with the adhesive burrs of the burr thistle (*Arctimus bardana*) that the total effect is that of a suit of chain armour. Arms, legs, body and face are all hidden by this prickly material, so that the wearer is altogether unrecognizable; only his eyes are visible through holes cut in the cloth to enable him to see. On his head, he has a cap, or helmet, of roses, and in each hand he carries a staff profusely decked with flowers.

At about 9.00 a.m. on Ferry Fair Eve, the Burryman starts out on his slow perambulation of the burgh, which does not end until late afternoon. He is accompanied by two attendants who wear ordinary, undecorated clothes; and usually they are all followed by a lively company of children and young people. He walks with his arms outstretched sideways carrying the flower staves, and his attendants, one on each side, help him to bear the weight by supporting the staff ends. He goes from house to house along the 7-mile route; as he comes to each one, a shout is raised and those within run out to greet him and bestow their gifts upon him. During all this the Burryman does not speak at all but stands in silence before the door, while the money given is collected in a can carried by his attendants.

Various theories have been put forward to account for this curious ceremony. One is that it commemorates the landing at South Queensferry of Queen Margaret, the saintly wife of King Malcolm Canmore, from whom the town derives its name. This was an important event in the history of the burgh and is recorded on its seal. But the peculiar nature of the Burryman himself suggests that he is far older than the eleventh-century queen, and is quite probably a relic of some pre-Christian figure connected with the harvest, or perhaps one transferred from the vegetation rites of May to a later date in the year. It is clear that his visits are still felt to be in some way luck-bringing and there is, or was, a tradition that if the custom was ever abandoned, it would bring misfortune to the town.

It is possible that the Burryman may once have played the part of the scapegoat. There is no record that he was ever driven out or sacrificed, though he was formerly believed to carry away the evils afflicting the community as he passed. At Buckie on the Moray Firth, when the fishing season was bad a man wearing a flannel shirt stuck all over with burrs was paraded through the village in a hand barrow, to bring better luck to the fishing. At Fraserburgh also, until the middle of last century, the fishermen chose one of their number to act as Burryman and 'raise the herring' when ordinary luck failed. He too wore garments covered with burrs and a hat with herrings hanging head downwards all round the brim. Thus attired he rode on horseback through the streets, preceded by a piper, and followed by a large and noisy crowd of fishermen and townspeople.

Queensferry is the gateway to Edinburgh on the southern shore of the Firth of Forth.

Nearest railway stations: Dalmeny and Edinburgh.

ST MARGARET'S HOPE, South Ronaldsay, Orkney

Ploughing the Sands
On one Wednesday in August, the boys

of the island engage in a mimic ploughing match on the beach. The contest used to take place at Easter but it was shifted in recent years, possibly to coincide with the tourist season.

Before the ploughing begins, the 'Horses' are judged. These are in fact island girls who compete with each other in the splendour of their costumes, whose style somewhat resembles the dress of the pearly kings and queens of London. When the finest costume has been settled upon, the crowd moves down to the beach and the ploughing begins. The Horses take no part in this and the boys have to work their miniature ploughs – which are often of ancient and beautiful workmanship – by themselves. The young ploughmen show great skill in turning unbroken, straight furrows in the smooth sand; when the best line has been judged, the day is ended with a party and prizegiving.

There are ferries and air services to the Orkneys from Aberdeen and Scrabster. But to ascertain the date of the contest, and details of inter-island ferries, it would be best to contact the Orkney Tourist Organization, Information Centre, Kirkwall, Orkney, before setting out.

STONEHAVEN, Grampian

Hogmanay Fireballs

Here on New Year's Eve the Old Year is burned out with fireballs. These are round balls of inflammable material soaked in tar and held in wire-netting cages on the end of long pieces of wire rope. They are carried by young men who appear at midnight and parade up and down the main street of the old town, swinging the blazing balls in great fiery arcs round their heads. The effect is both startling and exciting, but the whirling fireballs are not as dangerous as they look because of the practised skill of the performers in the manipulation of their long ropes.

Stonehaven, an old fishing port on the windy Mearns coast, is situated some 12 miles down the A92 from Aberdeen.

Nearest railway station: Stonehaven.

FURTHER READING

William W. Addison, *English Fairs and Markets*, Batsford, 1953

Violet Alford, *Introduction to English Folklore*, G. Bell, 1952

Batsford County Folklore Series, Batsford

E. C. Blunden, *English Villages*, Collins, 1941

Roy Christian, *Old English Customs*, Country Life, 1966

J. R. W. Coxhead, *Old Devon Customs*, Raleigh Press, 1957

W. T. Dennison, *Orkney Folklore and Tradition*, Herald Press

G. MacDonald Fraser, *The Steel Bonnets*, Barrie & Jenkins, 1971

Sir J. G. Frazer, *The Golden Bough*, MacMillan, 1936

Christina Hole, *Christmas and its Customs*, Richard Bell, 1957

Christina Hole, *Easter and its Customs*, Richard Bell, 1961

Christina Hole, *English Customs and Usage*, Batsford, 1942

Alexander Howard, *Endless Cavalcade*, Arthur Barker, 1964

H. Cecil Hunt, *British Customs and Ceremonies*, Ernest Benn, 1954

E. H. Carkeet James, *H.M. Tower of London*, Staple Press, 1953

T. Gwynn Jones, *Welsh Folklore and Folk Custom*, Methuen, 1930

Frank Muir, *Christmas Customs and Traditions*, Sphere, 1975

Venetia Newall, *An Egg at Easter*, Routledge, 1971

Iona and Peter Opie, *The Lore and Language of Schoolchildren*, Clarendon Press, 1959

Trefor M. Owen, *Welsh Folk Customs*, Welsh Folk Museum, 1959

C. I. Paton, *Manx Calendar Customs*, Folklore Society, 1942

Crichton Porteous, *The Beauty and Mystery of Well-Dressing*, Pilgrim Press, 1949

D. R. Rawe, *Padstow 'Obby Oss and May Day Festivities*, Lodenek Press, 1972

Reader's Digest, *Folklore, Myths and Legends of Britain*, Reader's Digest, 1973

Reader's Digest, *Illustrated Guide to Britain*, Reader's Digest, 1982

Hugh Rippon, *Discovering English Folk Dance*, Shire

Cecil Sharpe, *Sword Dance of Northern England*, Novello, 1913

Shell Guide to Scotland, Ebury Press & Rainbird, 1965

E. B. Simpson, *Folklore in Lowland Scotland*, Dent, 1908

USEFUL ADDRESSES

British Tourist Authority
Information Centre
64 St James's Street
London SW1A 1NF

English Tourist Board
4 Grosvenor Gardens
London SW1 0DU

Scottish Tourist Board
23 Ravelston Terrace
Edinburgh EH1 1BR

Wales Tourist Board
Brunel House
2 Fitzalan Road
Cardiff CF2 1UY

London Tourist Board
Platform 15
Victoria Station
London SW1

Cumbria Tourist Board
Ellerthwaite
Windermere
Cumbria

East Anglia Tourist Board
14 Museum Street
Ipswich, Suffolk
IP1 1HU

Heart of England Tourist Board
PO Box 15
Worcester WR1 2JT

North West Tourist Board
Last Drop Village
Bromley Cross
Bolton BL7 9PZ

South-east England Tourist Board
Cheviot House
4–6 Monson Road
Tunbridge Wells, Kent
TN1 1NH

Southern Tourist Board
The Old Town Hall
Leigh Road
Eastleigh, Hants
SO5 4DE

Thames and Chilterns Tourist Board
PO Box 10
8 The Market Place
Abingdon
Oxon OX14 3HG

West Country Tourist Board
Trinity Court
37 Southernhay East
Exeter, Devon
EX1 1QS

Yorkshire and Humberside Tourist
Board
312 Tadcaster Road
York YO2 2HF

City of Edinburgh District Council
5 Waverley Bridge
Edinburgh EH1 1BR

Borders Regional Council
Newtown
St Boswells, Roxburghshire
TD6 0SA

Dumfries and Galloway Tourist
  Association
Douglas House
Newton Stewart DG8 6DQ

Strathclyde Regional Council
McIver House
Cadogan Street
Glasgow G2 7QB

Tayside Regional Council
Tayside House
26–8 Crichton Street
Dundee DD1 3RD

Highlands and Islands Development
    Board
PO Box 7
Bridge House
Bank Street
Inverness

Mid Wales Tourism Council
The Owain Glendwr Centre
Machynlleth
Powys

North Wales Tourist Council
Civic Centre
Colwyn Bay
Clwyd

South Wales Tourism Council
Darkgate
Carmarthen
Dyfed

INDEX